"Reading *Real Life Intuition* felt like a wa̶ ̶ ̶ ̶ ̶ ̶ ̶ ̶ ̶ ̶ enlightening conversation with a good friend or many good friends. If you have ever wondered if you are intuitive, this book is for you. You *will* relate to these compelling, vivid, and amazing stories and discover plenty of exercises and tips on how to take your intuition to the next level."

—**SHERRIE DILLARD**, bestselling author of *I'm Still With You*

"Engaging, enlightening, and eclectic—all I can say is wow! In Melanie Barnum's new book, *Real Life Intuition*, not only will you benefit from her expert guidance as a professional intuitive, but you will recognize your own intuitive abilities through the experiences of others. This book is amazing, and honestly, I couldn't stop reading once I started because I wanted to read all of the different intuitive experiences. Some are very profound, many make you smile, and lots of them make you think, *Hey! That's happened to me too*, which is confirmation of your own intuitive abilities. *Real Life Intuition* is going to be a keeper that you'll refer back to and recommend to others again and again."

—**MELISSA ALVAREZ**, author of *Your Psychic Self* and *365 Ways to Raise Your Frequency*

"In this wonderful collection of intuitive stories by people from all walks of life, you may discover that you are more intuitive than you think.... This book provides a grounded and practical approach to developing and paying attention to our intuition—including definitions, lived experiences, things to ponder, and numerous exercises to strengthen your natural intuitive gifts.... This book is a perfect addition to anyone's collection and makes a great gift. Who knows, maybe your intuition led you to this book. If so, listen and see what happens."

—**GRANDDAUGHTER CROW**, author of *Wisdom of the Natural World*

REAL LIFE
INTUITION

About the Author

Melanie Barnum (Connecticut) is a psychic, medium, speaker, life coach, and hypnotist who has been practicing professionally for over twenty years. She is a multiple award-winning author whose books have been translated into several languages and has been featured in numerous print, broadcast, and online media bookings. Melanie's friendly and down-to-earth manner and gifted psychic insight make her readings unique and powerful, providing invaluable advice and guidance related to relationships, family, career, and educational opportunities. She has facilitated her clients' communication with their spiritual guides and deceased loved ones. In addition, she offers mentorship, guidance, and support for those interested in developing their intuitive abilities. For more, visit MelanieBarnum.com.

Author of *The Book of Psychic Symbols*

REAL LIFE
INTUITION

Extraordinary Stories
from People Who Listen
to Their Inner Voice

MELANIE BARNUM

Llewellyn Publications
Woodbury, Minnesota

FIRST EDITION
First Printing, 2024

Cover design by Kevin R. Brown

Llewellyn Publications is a registered trademark of Llewellyn Worldwide Ltd.

Library of Congress Cataloging-in-Publication Data (Pending)
ISBN: 978-0-7387-7545-6

Llewellyn Worldwide Ltd. does not participate in, endorse, or have any authority or responsibility concerning private business transactions between our authors and the public.

All mail addressed to the author is forwarded but the publisher cannot, unless specifically instructed by the author, give out an address or phone number.

Any internet references contained in this work are current at publication time, but the publisher cannot guarantee that a specific location will continue to be maintained. Please refer to the publisher's website for links to authors' websites and other sources.

Llewellyn Publications
A Division of Llewellyn Worldwide Ltd.
2143 Wooddale Drive
Woodbury, MN 55125-2989
www.llewellyn.com

Printed in the United States of America

Other Works by Melanie Barnum

The Book of Psychic Symbols
Intuition at Work
Llewellyn's Little Book of Psychic Development
Manifest Your Year
Psychic Abilities for Beginners
Psychic Development Beyond Beginners
Psychic Symbols Oracle Cards
Psychic Vision
The Steady Way to Greatness

Featured In

Mastering Magick
The Secret Psychic
365 Days of Angel Prayers

Dedication

My family. 'Nuff said.

For real, though. My family; my rocks, my best friends. Tom, my husband, Molly, my oldest, and Samantha, my youngest—they are there for me. When it comes time to send in my manuscript, we get together and do a little hand gesture, creating magick, and we all yell "Bloop bloop bloop" continuously until the email goes through! They support and love that I am an author and already are asking what the next book is going to be!

There is nothing better than feeling supported and loved through the process of writing a manuscript, no matter what the book is actually about. They get it. They all do!

My sister, Tammy Nelson, also an author and best friend, deserves a shoutout. She continually checks in and tells me, when those days come around that I feel stressed about my looming deadline, "You've got this!"

Finally, thanks to my friends! They are probably all getting sick of hearing me say, "I can't today, have to write!" But again, they are all there to raise me up when I sometimes feel like I'll never finish.

This book is dedicated to all of them. Without the love they share with me, I don't know that I'd be able to keep doing what I love, and man, do I love it!

Contents

Acknowledgments

THANK YOU!!!

There is no way I'd ever be able to write this book without the stories shared with me by people from every walk of life. From students to police officers to doctors to authors and everyone in between, THANK YOU! You shared your beliefs and your intuitive moments, and I can't express my appreciation enough! There have been so many incredible conversations that began with "Oh, I don't think I've got anything. I don't really use my intuition" but ended with "Oh, there was this one time…" Their stories are here. Written for you and all of us who believe in the magic of intuition.

I can't list everyone who contributed, but know that I am beyond grateful for you all! Not only have you provided the anecdotes and narratives that seem so unbelievable but are real life intuition, you have also shared true parts of your lives with me to send out to the world. Intuition, an often-doubted gift, is real. With so many extrasensory accounts, it's impossible not to believe that our gifts, our vibes, our metaphysical messages are, in fact, accessible to everyone.

My new friends I met while sharing and celebrating our mutual wins at the COVR awards—your words of wisdom and your belief that I deserved to be there inspired me and helped me look at my work through the eyes of (other) professionals. For this, I am extremely grateful!

And I couldn't finish this without acknowledging Llewellyn Worldwide. The publishing house that has been with me since day one! I will miss my acquisitions editor and friend, Angela Wix, but welcomed the opportunity to work with Amy Glaser again, and welcome Nicole Borneman!

Again, just acknowledging you all isn't enough—you are all amazing and so incredibly generous to help me and all of my books succeed! Hope you enjoy *Real Life Intuition*!

Disclaimer

The practices and techniques described in this book should not be used as an alternative to professional medical treatment. This book does not attempt to give medical diagnoses, treatments, prescriptions, or suggestions for medication in relation to any human disease, pain, injury, deformity, or physical or mental condition.

The author and publisher of this book are not responsible in any manner whatsoever for any injury that may occur through following the examples contained herein. It is recommended that you consult your physician to obtain a diagnosis for any physical or mental symptoms you may experience.

While the author intends for you to enjoy the stories contained within and learn how to use your own intuition, this book makes no guarantee that you will increase your intuitive abilities by following the recommended practices.

The stories shared in this book are based on real life events and readings. Many of the names and some of the circumstances have been changed to preserve privacy.

INTRODUCTION

Within the pages of this book, you will find some seemingly ordinary and many extraordinary stories of real life intuition, from real people. Sometimes their intuition surprised them, and other times they recognized it for what it was: their natural, inherent ability to tune in to the universal energy that connects us all. Whether or not they were aware of their gifts previously, you'll likely connect to at least a few of their stories. You will also have the opportunity to practice using your own intuition through the book's exercises.

Above all, I ask that you read this with an open mind. Allow yourself to relate to the accounts that others have been excited—and, sometimes, brave enough—to share with you!

EXERCISE Protection

Before doing any of the exercises in the book, you'll want to protect yourself from any negativity. It's important to note that throughout this book, I will talk about where and how the information is coming through; in all circumstances, I am talking about positive energy, never negative energy or energies. Feel free to repeat this exercise as you continue exploring your own gifts.

Get into a comfy position and just begin breathing, in and out. Inhale positive vibes, exhale nonsense and negativity you no longer need. Then, imagine a screen (like a window screen) growing all around you, made of beautiful light. This screen will allow positive messages and helpful information to come through, while keeping you safe from anything that would harm you or cause you grief in any way.

This screen can grow larger with every breath, encompassing your body, the room you are in, and even your entire home. You can also choose to extend your protective screen to your family and friends. This protection is limited only by your belief that it is protecting you and those you designate in your circle. Keep it there as long as you want, but definitely invoke this screen before every exercise you do!

Intuition: We All Have It

We begin life with a knowing that we are connected, an intuitive awareness that we are capable of so much. Then, we discover that everything we knew when we came into this world may not have been right or, more importantly, may not have been widely accepted or recognized by society as valid—until, usually years later, we begin to understand that we were on the right track, and we are connected and capable of moving into our greatness, or at the very least, our happiness. What stops us from a natural progression from birth to intuition? Simple: we do.

Unfortunately, even well-intentioned people tend to stray from relying on or even using their intuitive gifts. But intuition is our birthright. It is the one thing that can truly help us move toward joy, but we shove it down and keep it hidden because the reality is it is intangible, and intangibles are difficult to prove. So, instead, we focus on the tangibles, those things we can grasp physically or see with our own eyes; they are the things we can all agree are real. Intuition is harder to verify.

However, that intuitive ability, that gift, comes around when you need it. It is a gut instinct, a feeling deep down—a knowing, even—about something, anything that you may be connected to, that, when it happens, makes you say "Aha!" or brings you comfort. We turn to our intuitive impressions when we need to decide something, when rational thought has run its course, or when we need help from someone other than those in the physical realm. We can call it prayer, or we can call it heavenly intervention, or we can call it what it is: a request sent out to the universe to help us in the best and most positive way. That is not to say that belief in a higher power is void or irrelevant. Belief in a higher power works. Because, and I don't say this lightly, the universal energy that you may identify as God, Jesus, Buddha, Mother Mary, or any other religious deity helps us connect to our own higher self and our intuition.

Again, it's that intuitive gift that most of us lose along the way because we've been told it's not real. But it finds its way back to us in times of need, and then we can learn to develop it and use it for so much more. Your intuition is yours and yours alone to rediscover and use to your benefit, and maybe even the benefit of others.

Who I Am

Even though I have always been intuitive, I didn't feel like it was a profession that went beyond the stereotypical scarf-wearing psychics on the boardwalk that have a reputation of being fake. I was so wrong. Now, I'm totally at ease with what I do.

I am an international award-winning author, a professional psychic, a healer, and a teacher. That's my current resume, summed up quite easily. But my background is so much more. I was a public accountant, preparing taxes for others. After that, I was the controller of a company. And I owned a children's boutique. Bet you weren't expecting that! So, how did that change? How did I end up somewhere so different from where I started? I had what I refer to as "intuitive guidance"—and I needed to be hit over the head to listen to it.

One day, shortly after I had my first daughter, when I was still working as the controller of a company, using mostly my left brain, I actually felt like I was hit over the head. Nothing too hard, but intense enough for me to pay attention to it. And I heard the words *You need to do this work now*. That was it! That was my life-changing event. And to anyone else, it might sound like I made it up, or even—and forgive me for saying it—it might seem a bit crazy. But I knew in that moment, when I heard those words, that it was real.

Being metaphysically hit over the head decades ago was the wake-up call I needed to use my birthright, my intuition. But this book is not just my coming-out story as a professional psychic. It is so much more. This is real life—my life, and the lives of others. This book is a collection of stories from people who describe themselves as normal, everyday people—people who have accepted that using their intuition is indeed natural and, as a matter of fact, it is helpful! Imagine that.

Who We All Are

We are creators. We are doers. We are thinkers. We are people. In that way, we are all similar. We need food and water to survive, some form of interaction. That's what makes us human. But we are also all unique. There is not one single person that is exactly you, *except* you.

We all have interests, and most of us have things in life that we feel drawn to. We won't all have the same interests or be excited by the same things. We may have some commonalities, but we also have many differences, and that's what builds strong communities and schools and societies in general. This is fantastic, because the world needs everyone, from garbage collectors to scientists, from musicians to accountants, from doctors to sculptors, and everything in between. We need everyone to function, to keep us going as a civilization. Whether we want to or not, we all play a role. So why not make our contribution something that not only helps the group as a whole, but also makes us excited to wake up in the morning? Why not imagine we can have and be more?

Imagination. That is where our dreams live: early goals of being firefighters or movie stars or ballerinas or professional athletes—all those things we thought of when we were little, things we forgot about because we were told they weren't realistic … Those are our dreams that went to die. But the thing is, our childhood dreams have a lot to teach us. Most people have visions of who they want to be or emulate when they're younger because they are drawn to a certain path. For instance, the kid who wanted to be a firefighter may be drawn to helping others. The child who wanted to be a movie star might find themselves wanting to be a teacher or lecturer, or another profession where they are regularly in the spotlight. So often, though, we abandon our dreams for practical reasons: we have to support ourselves and, eventually, our family. We give up on our dreams for more real-world endeavors. And this is not a terrible thing. However, we have the power to achieve so much more.

When we turn inward, or even to the heavens, and ask for guidance, what we receive back is usually a muted intuitive sense, and if we are smart, we listen to it. We explore it. We consider it to be more than just imagination. And that is the beginning, an opening to what could be a whole new life. Learning to trust that feeling—that vision in the mind's eye—might take a while. That's okay. Often, it's a process. It's important to investigate it further. It's crucial to believe intuition is real in order to follow it.

So, ask for validation. Request additional intuitive impressions until you believe that you are actually experiencing intuitive guidance. Question it until you believe it's real. That's when you can really start using your intuition to your benefit. Open up to your gifts; expand your career (and your life in general) by tapping into the metaphysical senses you're born with.

The Metaphysical

The word *metaphysical* can be used to describe intuitive sciences or philosophy. It can conjure thoughts of spirituality or supernatural occurrences. *Mystical*, *esoteric*, and even *abstract* are more words that come to mind when describing the metaphysical. All of these explain bits and pieces of what metaphysical means. To me, it is not simply the unknown, but the other side of the physical: that which can't always be touched; the metaphysical is a way to look at fundamentally beneficial aspects of our lives from a different perspective.

But there is no reason to label it if that causes you distress. It need not even be named, because as I said, it's always been there—naming it doesn't change that. Just know that addressing the metaphysical as an opportunity to tune in to your intuition is the scariest it needs to be. And the only thing frightening about that is the realization that your life may change for the better once you do!

Let's face it: if you're not scared away yet, you probably won't be. Chances are, if you've read this far, you are open—perhaps even excited—to hear stories from real people who have discovered their incredible gifts in a way that has helped them and, sometimes, others. They've believed that intuition is real and have taken it a step further by actually using the soul impressions they received to further their lives, sometimes in extraordinary ways.

As you'll soon see, intuitive messages are not always dramatic. You don't have to be metaphysically hit over the head to realize your intuition is talking to you (unless, of course, you're like I was so long ago). In this book, you'll learn what intuitive messages can mean and how the people who received them were able to interpret and utilize them. And, of course, there will be Exercises, Ponder This moments, and Pro Tips to help you discover your own natural gifts, and to help you develop your abilities further.

Before we begin, a final note: the stories contained in this book were given freely, without coercion, because the contributors wanted to share their experiences. Often, they explained to me that they wanted readers to know how important it is to follow and believe in gut instincts, because when it comes right down to it, that's all we have. Our instincts are born from intuition, and we have survived since the days of cave dwelling by using our instincts. We had no choice then. It was simple: move on to the next cave when you get a nagging sensation that you're about to be eaten by a lion, or stay and be an appetizer. Animals are the same; they rely on their physical senses, but also their metaphysical, intuitive senses. We are so much more than animals now.

Chapter 1

WHAT INTUITION IS

Intuition is a feeling, a knowing, a nudge toward realizing that something beyond our five physical senses is happening, which allows us to become aware of or notice something or someone without evidential, tangible proof. It is a natural and often-underrated sensory input that we use on a daily basis, though we don't always recognize it. Intuition is a gift that is often overlooked or doubted until we decide to embrace our extrasensory selves.

Everyone—and I do mean *everyone*—has intuitive moments. What is interesting is we don't always remember them, especially if we don't acknowledge them in the moment. We also don't always recognize these moments when we have them. I am a professional psychic, and this I know: I don't always follow my gut instincts. I should, and I tell everyone else they should. But I'm human, and I sometimes disregard my intuition.

You may question this, and I don't really blame you. I question it too. I am fully aware that I am a walking contradiction. Some may say I'm hypocritical. However, I believe I'm just living my human existence, as we all are. When I'm not working and intentionally tuning in, I dampen my psychic abilities so as not to be overwhelmed. This is common for many people, regardless of whether they are intentionally shutting down or doing it without understanding they are stifling their gifts. When we do this, though, it can cause us to discount our gifts. For example, when I'm at the grocery store and walk by the milk and think, *I should grab some*, but I continue without putting it in the cart because I know I have some at home, I am ignoring my intuition. I'm not listening to my soul's guidance, but I'm not aware of this until I get home and discover I just ran out of milk.

Ignoring metaphysical tingles or snubbing those intuitive nudges may keep us from expanding our awareness. We do need to listen to our sixth sense, often, which also means we need to learn *how* to do that. Learning to tap into your metaphysical senses can assist you when trying to understand other people. As a professional, I pay attention to the messages I receive from my own intuition, my higher self, my soul, as well as my helpers: spirit guides and deceased loved ones.

As I stated earlier, when we need assistance, we send out requests to the universe. It is the same process with the psychic readings I give. I send out requests to receive impressions from what I call *universal energy*, and I open up to positive source—usually, that means a combination of my helpers along with my client's helpers. Helpers send messages to us that we need to interpret using our intuition. Sometimes those messages are clear, but most times they need to be translated. When your spirit guides and deceased loved ones show up for you, they are counting on you to use your own intuition to illuminate the messages they are conveying.

Sometimes we feel things, see things, or even know things, but we don't put together that this may be the result of our metaphysical senses. This is one of the biggest reasons people ignore their intuition. Once you realize you may be keeping yourself from tuning in, it becomes easier to pay attention. You begin to recognize those aha moments when your senses are talking to you, and then you can learn to interpret what those impressions mean.

In my endeavors to create this book, many people I asked to contribute initially responded with, "I'm not sure if I've had any intuitive experiences." That usually changed within a couple of minutes once they remembered their experiences. We may not always have huge aha moments that are easily recalled, but everyone has moments of intuition on a weekly basis, if not daily. When we don't recognize them for what they are, they kind of get buried in the deep recesses of the brain. However, when you have a big aha moment, you tend to remember it easily, whether you are aware it's your intuition or not.

Intuitive moments, even the not-so-strong moments, occur often. But at times, it's harder to recognize them for what they are because they don't always happen in a way that feels familiar. So, what does that mean? Simply put, it means your intuition tries to get your attention for the big and little things in life, and understanding how it works will help open your eyes to your own metaphysical gifts.

Explaining Intuitive Gifts

There are no magic beans involved when it comes to intuition or intuitive gifts. The magic is what we are able to discover when we pay attention to our ESP, or extrasensory perception. We don't always ask for it. In fact, most of the time, we don't set out to use it! However, it shows up in a variety of ways to help us. Some of the most common metaphysical gifts are clairsentience, clairvoyance, clairaudience, claircognizance, clairolfaction, and clairgustance. If you are like me, stories can add to understanding how each ability may present, so I've shared some here that will help you grasp how these metaphysical abilities can appear in our lives.

Clairsentience

The feeling you have when your intuition is trying to get your attention is one of the most common forms of intuitive awareness, and it's called clairsentience, or clear feeling. Generally referred to as your gut instinct, it helps you know when something is right or wrong, when you should stay or leave, or even which direction you should go. These gut instincts also help you in times of danger.

Margaret

For my client Margaret, a moment of clairsentience happened when she was nineteen. She had bought her first brand-new vehicle at seventeen, a Jeep Wrangler. She was beyond psyched, having purchased this cool car with her own money, back when there weren't as many on the road. She loved it…until she felt there was something wrong with it.

So, she brought it to the service area of the dealership. They looked it over and promptly told her there was nothing wrong. She persisted, to the point of bringing it in five times, to no avail. Finally, feeling in her gut there *was* something wrong with it, she decided she needed to get rid of it.

Two days after she traded in her Jeep, someone purchased it. It had low mileage, and it still looked brand new. It was an easy sell. However, there was one pesky little issue. The salesman called her the next week.

"I was just wondering, was there anything wrong with the Jeep when you turned it in?" he asked.

Turns out, the person who bought it was driving off the lot and the carburetor blew up. The whole front end of the Jeep went up in flames. The driver made it out unscathed, thankfully. Margaret felt validated that her intuition had helped her do the right thing. She had trusted her gut instincts. She had imagined disaster, but she listened to her intuition and averted it.

Clairvoyance

Intuition is not always something you feel in your gut; there are many different ways to experience it. Seeing things in your mind's eye (or with your third eye, as it's sometimes referred to) is known as clairvoyance. Most people who experience this type of intuitive guidance will see flashes of an image internally when they have a clairvoyant episode. Some will feel as though they are watching someone or something live, in action. But most often, when seeing something intuitively, it will appear like a photograph, a moment captured in time, a brief impression of something either literal or symbolic.

My third eye helped me out right after we bought our family's new home. When we were initially looking, I had tuned in to my intuition and received a plethora of information about our soon-to-be house. Then, we closed on it. I thought that would be it. However, I began seeing other images in my mind. I saw an image of my grandmother's house, which was totally different from ours. It had dark, aged cedar shingle siding whereas ours had been re-sided in tan vinyl. I also saw a beautiful stone fireplace but, in our new family home, we only had a wood-burning stove. On top of those images, I saw a cottage—a smaller house—as well, which we definitely did not have on the current property.

When I told my husband what I was seeing, he replied, "Absolutely not! We are not moving again," although he knew by then that when I saw something or had some type of intuitive flash, it was meaningful.

After a quick series of events that included a boat ride and a phone call about a "For Sale" sign we saw on a lake house, we ended up at the realtor's listing. There, in all its glory, was a house that looked just like my grandmother's, with the same aged, brown cedar siding. We could see a beautiful stone fireplace rising up the outside of the home. We also saw the cottage, directly in front of us. It needed work but was currently being rented.

I looked at Tom, and we didn't even have to go inside. "We'll take it," he said. He knew it was the image I had shared with him. We bought it less than a year after having moved, which otherwise would have made no sense whatsoever, but we knew when my intuition talked, there was no ignoring it. It became our lake house, a vacation home that we have since completely renovated and rented out as our kids grew older. Now, my older daughter is happily living her dream in the cottage. It was meant to be.

Many people ask me, "If you have clairsentient abilities or clairvoyance, are you restricted to just one? Can you have both? Or even other senses?" Of course you can! There is no limit to what intuitive senses you may experience, though many people notice one sense is generally stronger than the others.

Clairaudience

Clairaudience is clear hearing. Many people who are drawn to music or some form of public speaking may find intuitive hearing becomes their first connection to metaphysical awareness.

Joy

Joy came to me one day because she needed help. "I keep hearing words and I have no idea where they're coming from—I feel like I'm going crazy!" she told me.

"What are you hearing?" I asked her.

"Directions or something. I'm hearing 'stop' or 'go' and other things like that," she continued.

Believe it or not, I am very skeptical. Yup, I said it. I don't look to the metaphysical first; I always try to find a practical reason for what someone is experiencing. However, this definitely sounded like Joy's intuition trying to guide her.

"Are you by chance thinking of anything in particular when you hear these directions?" I questioned.

"I suppose so. It happened yesterday. I was thinking about whether to leave my job or not. I mean, I like my job, but I just wonder if there's something more for me out there."

There it was. Her intuition was actively trying to help her. She shared she was a teacher at a middle school, and she taught English.

I knew there was more to it, so I prodded, "And is that what you always wanted to do?"

"No. I went to school with a double major—teaching and music. I'd love to teach music to either middle schoolers or high school students," she replied dreamily.

Before I asked, I already knew the answer. "And when you're thinking about whether to change jobs, what do you hear?"

"Well, I suppose I hear 'go!'" Joy told me with a faraway look in her eyes.

She sat, stunned into silence. It was a breakthrough moment. She knew immediately, after our short conversation, what was happening. She wasn't crazy. It was her intuition talking to her. It was time for her to make the shift and start doing what she'd always wanted to do. All she needed was validation from me to listen and pay attention to the words she was hearing.

Joy had discovered what was probably her most prevalent intuitive ability: clairaudience. What she may not have realized is she was also using a bit of another metaphysical sense—claircognizance. She knew she needed to change her career. Not just because she longed for it, but also because she felt in her bones, deep down, that it was what she needed to do. She wasn't listening to her intuition, so she was given more guidance. The words she heard were what finally pushed her to come to me, and ultimately to change her career. In Joy's case, it wasn't a huge career change on paper; she would still be a teacher. But to her, it would change her quality of life. Once she was able to make the move, she found she enjoyed life again and actually looked forward to going to work every day.

Claircognizance

Claircognizance is an intuitive knowing. Clear knowing. It's knowing something as fact, though you have no earthly reason to know it. It's a profound certainty for which you have no evidence or proof, but you know without a doubt it is truth. It's an honest, legitimate conviction that what you're feeling is absolutely real, even though you can't verify it in the physical world … yet.

This clear knowing was evident for me many years ago. One particular episode comes to mind. My husband and I went out with a group of friends. We were having a great time, indulging in some appetizers and drinks at a local bar. We were in the side room and pretty much had the area to ourselves. The restaurant had a pool table, so we all took turns playing games. We were ordering another round of drinks when, unexpectedly, I knew we had to leave.

Turning to Tom, who had already had his fair share of vodka, I said, "We need to go, and we need to go right now."

As per usual after drinking, he told me he really wanted fast food. "Please. We need food."

Knowing he had overindulged and that he was craving greasy, comforting burgers and fries, I gave in. I had another nagging feeling that we shouldn't go straight home, even though it was close to the bar, right around the corner, and the drive-thru was in the next town over. For some strange reason, I had a feeling that being farther away from the bar was a good idea.

Fortunately for us, on our way back home, we received a group text message about what had happened after we left. Apparently, our friends had been jumped by a group of young, buzzed twenty-somethings who had come in to play pool and were mad that our friends were taking too long. The twenty-somethings got loud and threw the first punch, along with a couple of chairs. This is just one example of a time I mercifully listened to my intuition, which hadn't just nudged me, but demanded I pay attention immediately.

I credit all of my intuitive abilities for the positive direction I go in life. I know for a fact that if I ignore my sometimes-not-so-gentle guidance, things will not turn out the way I'd like. It's not that life itself will come to an end or that horrible outcomes will always happen, but it just seems to make life harder when I discount the vibes I pick up, no matter how they happen. Intuition is not always cut and dried. Occasionally, I pick up on changes in the ambience or the atmosphere; perhaps this has happened to you as well. Though not always evident that it's our otherworldly gifts, you can rest assured that is exactly what is transpiring.

Clairolfaction/Clairalience

Clairolfaction or clairalience is another intuitive ability that appears to change the air around you. It is the gift of psychic smell or scent. It's pretty common for people to share they have smelled their deceased grandmother's special perfume or their father's cigars from the other side. These can be happy events, as we often welcome these encounters because we miss our loved ones. The experience Ray had, however, was not the same.

Ray

Ray had a cool apartment that he had lived in for about two years. It wasn't your average apartment; it was the top two floors of a house, and his landlords lived right downstairs. When Ray's roommate decided to move out at the end of their lease, he debated whether to get another roommate and extend his lease or move out and find a new place.

Initially, he decided he wanted to stay because he liked his apartment. Then, he began smelling a strange odor, and it got stronger every time he imagined himself staying. It smelled like charcoal and was permeating his senses—it only went away when he thought about moving out. Ray saw this as a warning: *get out or something bad is going to happen!* He decided to leave. Once he moved out, he realized he no longer smelled the burning scent.

A few days after he left, his old landlords called him and asked if he had experienced anything strange in the kitchen. It turned out the second and third floor of the house—his apartment—had caught on fire. Apparently, there were wires inside the kitchen wall that were old. The firefighters told them they had shorted out and caught fire. Thank goodness no one was living there.

Even more fortunate was that directly above Ray's kitchen was the living room, and he'd had a large piano. If he was still there, the fire would have caused that piano to fall through the floor into the kitchen, then down into the first floor of the landlord's home—the space below Ray's old kitchen was the landlords' infant daughter's room.

The landlords' apartment on the first floor was unscathed by the fire. Unfortunately, it was necessary to rebuild the house due to smoke and water damage. The smell Ray had been sensing with his intuition was undoubtedly the scent of the embers from the fire to come.

Clairgustance

It's quite common to smell and taste together. Food tastes better when you can smell it; it enhances the flavor experience. These senses help each other. The same is true with clairolfaction and clairgustance, or clear taste.

Every year there's a carnival in our town. They have typical carnival food and rides. A few years back, my husband and I decided to swing by and grab some food for dinner. Now, usually I make sure to ask my kids if they want anything. This time, however, I hadn't. I didn't think they were going to be home, so I didn't bother.

Tom and I ate there, then left to head home. As soon as we walked in, my daughter asked, "Did you guys eat at the carnival and not ask me if I wanted anything?"

Right away I thought she must smell it on us. But nope, I was wrong. It was better than that. The looks we had on our faces gave it away. She knew she was right.

"Did you just finish? Because about a half hour ago I started tasting pulled pork and corn on the cob. Did you also have fried Oreos?"

I just stood there dumbfounded. She'd nailed it—that's exactly what we ate. But she didn't get the cotton candy–flavored milkshake.

"And, what's with the cotton candy that's not cotton candy?" she continued.

No doubt she had tuned in to us through her clairgustance. She was tasting what we had. Her taste buds were pretty good at discerning flavors, too! Obviously, my daughter forgave us for not bringing her food; she just wanted to make us squirm a bit. However, it further supported her belief that she had a pretty strong metaphysical sense. It also confirmed my belief that I wouldn't be able to hide too much from her!

Other Means to Receive Intuitive Messages

There are so many ways intuition can present. From determining which direction to go to keeping people safe and everything in between, this sixth sense is part of your life and always will be, regardless of whether you take advantage of it or not.

Humans are so busy. We are frequently overstimulated. We are working or we are parenting; watching television or listening to music; reading books or scanning the latest status updates from our friends and even strangers on social media. This has, for many of us, become the norm. Intuition sometimes has a hard time getting through to us during our waking moments because we don't have a moment to stop and pay attention to what our metaphysical senses are trying to share with us.

Qualifying how your intuition may show up helps you recognize your gifts in different ways. When your mind is working hard, you can easily miss the intuitive nudges that are trying to get your attention. Thankfully, your intuition also works hard, and it can offer you a multitude of opportunities to tune in to your ESP.

Dreams

People often write to me about dreams they've had. Once, a woman wrote to me about a dream that her brakes had given out, causing an accident. She emailed to ask for my psychic advice.

"Did the dream feel like it was fake, and you barely remember it? Or do you remember every bit of it, down to the smallest detail?" I probed.

"It felt real. I recall the car I hit; like I remember the color, the make, and even the driver. I also know it was morning time. I can still feel how the brake pedal went all the way to the floor before the accident," she replied.

I explained I thought she'd had an intuitive warning through her dream, and she might want to pay attention to it. She said she would have her brakes checked out, though she hadn't heard any telltale squeaking, which is a clue it might be time to change the brake pads.

She messaged me about a week later.

"I had my boyfriend check out my brakes. At first, he said there was nothing wrong with the pads. They were still almost new. But then, he pressed down on the brake pedal and said, 'You know, something feels kind of funny.' He looked at the master cylinder and realized the fluid was super low. Then, he had me step on the brakes while he looked under the car. Sure enough, there was a leak in the brake line. If I had driven it again, I probably wouldn't have been able to stop."

Another crisis averted. But it wasn't *my* intuition that saved her. It was her dream, or possibly, it was a visitation from a deceased loved one, reaching out to her in her dream because she wasn't available to process her intuition during her waking moments. Either way, it was her choice whether to trust her dream as a portent of things to come. Thankfully, she did. Dreaming of a collision was enough to get her to slow down and heed the warning, and her dream ultimately prevented an accident.

Deceased Loved Ones

Deceased loved ones definitely have a habit of popping by to help us in various life endeavors. Occasionally, we are able to recognize they are coming through, but more often than not, we are unaware they are there. Our loved ones show up in many different ways: dreams, visions, scents, tastes, sounds, feelings, nudges, and anything else you could possibly imagine. They often send us intuitive messages through our clair senses.

Though cliché, deceased loves one might appear to us as something we associate with them, such as pennies or dragonflies or cardinals. For example, my mom comes to me as a monarch butterfly—so cliché it's almost laughable, but I know it's a little reminder that my mom is around. She especially shows up when I'm feeling down. When I see that telltale orange and black "flutter-by," as she called them, it's her cheering me up, letting me know there are better times ahead. Cliché is cliché for a reason: if something happens regularly, there's no denying it.

Signs and Synchronicities

This, of course, brings us to signs and synchronicities. I bet you've heard of them. You may have blown off their existence as nonsense, but I'm pretty sure all of us have had these intuitive moments. You may have even asked for a sign: *Please give a sign if I'm supposed to* ... And then we wait for that sign, questioning every possible sign that comes along because we need to be *sure* that was indeed the sign.

Synchronicities can be a bit trickier. They are signs or moments that you need to connect in order to identify them as synchronicities. These synchronistic events occur more frequently once you begin to understand what they are—messages your intuition, your guides, or other helpers are sending you. They are commonly referred to as coincidences. There's nothing wrong with that, but I also know that nine times out of ten, these "coincidences" are happening for a reason: to help you, to guide you, or just to make you say, "Huh. That was interesting." Coincidences allow you to distinguish between something meaningful and some random, unconnected thing that means absolutely nothing to you.

Understanding the Soul's Guidance

Frequently, a strong yearning is your intuition telling you there's more out there for you to learn or enjoy. You'll find that there are times when yearning is simply about wanting something because you desire it. But when you're yearning for life-altering changes, it's generally your intuitive voice trying to communicate with you.

It's common to have more than one intuitive sense guiding you, especially if you're not following the initial directive. If you're misinterpreting intuitive messages, or if you doubt what they're conveying, your soul tries to help another way. If you feel a sense of yearning, pay attention to it.

· · · · · · — · · · · · ·
PONDER THIS
ABILITIES

There is a quick way to determine which psychic ability you may use, even if you don't realize it: pay attention to the words you say. You might find yourself saying certain phrases often. These phrases can point you toward related metaphysical senses.

- **Claircognizance:** "I knew you were going to say that!" or "I knew that was going to happen!"
- **Clairsentience:** "I could feel that was going to happen!" or "I feel your pain!"
- **Clairvoyance:** "I see your point!" or "I can see how that happened!"
- **Clairaudience:** "I hear you!" or "It sounds to me like we should!"
- **Clairgustance:** "This is leaving a bad taste in my mouth!" or "Something tastes sour about that!"

+ **Clairalience:** "Something smells fishy!" or "I smell what you're cooking up!"

Obviously, some of these are common expressions, but you get the idea. By now, I'm willing to bet you've identified some (or, at the very least, one) intuitive gifts you've experienced.

By reading this entire chapter, you're more open to the possibility that the old version of what you thought to be real has gone out the window, along with all those other ideas you may have held on to. Now, though, you know (if you didn't already) that this thing called intuition, which shows itself in so many different ways, is real. It's not some fluffy, made-up idea or a crazy ideology you have to subscribe to, and it's definitely not a metaphysical cult for which you have to sign your life away in order to benefit. Nope. It's just intuition. Plain old intuition. But ain't it grand?

- ◉ -
PRO TIP

Intuition is our birthright and a normal part of life.

Chapter 2
CLAIRSENTIENCE AND CLAIREMPATHY

Clairsentience and clairempathy are often blurred together and can be difficult to differentiate between. The differences are occasionally so slight that they may seem to be the same clair gift. In their basic forms, clairsentience is feeling things about situations, people, or places. Clairempathy is more of an empathic feeling: intuitively feeling what someone else feels, or feeling the emotions of a specific person, present or not. Recognizing which of these intuitive perceptions you are tapping into, although possible, isn't always necessary—it's more about the experience of using your metaphysical senses.

I find people often use the word *empathetic* when what they are really experiencing is clairempathy. When you listen to someone share something they went through, you might be listening with an empathetic ear, but if you randomly feel another's emotions, you can attribute that more to your clairempathic senses.

Clairsentience

Clairsentience: we all have it. You may call it a hunch, a gut feeling, or just a stirring inside of you that tells you to pay attention, to heed a warning, to stop and take a breath before you continue what you're doing. It can also be that tingle inside that lets you know something or someone is great and should be explored further.

This is the most prevalent intuitive sense that can be attributed to daily life: Throughout the day, you make decisions. You don't always think about why you're choosing what you do, but every so often, you pick up a certain vibe that influences your choice. And, sometimes, you absolutely make conscious decisions because of the gentle soul guidance you receive.

Angela Wix

Angela Wix is an editor as well as an award-winning author of *The Secret Psychic*, and she has contributed to numerous metaphysical and healing books. She shared how her clairsentience helped her change her collegiate experience:

> When I was in my early twenties, I realized my intuition was guiding me to some unknown destination. I actually became more aware of it when an academic advisor called it out to me. We'd been discussing a switch in my undergraduate focus. I'd originally enrolled with a major in elementary education, something many of my friends had done—a quiet feeling told me it wasn't the right direction, but logically it seemed like a smart choice. Still, the more I resisted, the louder the feeling got, until it manifested in very uncomfortable ways.

Eventually, after weeks of going to bed with racing anxiety and horrible stomachaches, I finally switched to a double major in English and art. Then again, after a year of college, I was once again sensing that same nudging feeling, this time about changing my minor. I was listening to it with less resistance this second time around and was considering switching from humanities to graphic design. Unknowingly, I had been tapping in to reach my goals."

—Angela A. Wix

Angela's story is a great example of following our metaphysical instincts even when we don't understand that's what we are doing, or even *why* we're doing what we are doing. Have you ever had one of those moments when you have no idea why you're doing something, but it just feels like you should do it? I know I have. Usually, the reason will make itself clear at some point.

Alice

Alice, a waitress, woke up Saturday morning and looked outside at the beautiful weather. She decided to take a few friends out for a boat day on the lake. The day just kept getting better: the sun was shining, the water was warm and crystal clear—well, as clear as lake water is. Alice had packed the "big momma tube" so her and her friends could go tubing. It was like a giant mattress on the water and kept everyone from falling off, for the most part.

After they tubed, Alice and her friends alternated activities for the rest of the day, anchoring for a time and just floating, soaking up the rays. Then, they shook it up a bit and went around the lake *fast*, hitting the waves and laughing. They also pulled up to an island and had a picnic and a few drinks. The sun was nearing its down time, so they figured they were too, and they set off on the twenty-minute trip back to the dock.

Dusk was creeping up on them as Alice pulled the boat in, nose-first as usual. But, out of nowhere, she had a strange feeling she should back into the slip instead. She apologized to everyone and told them to hang on a minute as she turned the boat around, tying it up stern to dock. It took a little longer to get all of the covers snapped down properly because she wasn't used to the procedure that way, but her friends helped. Alice wondered to herself all the way home what had made her back in, and when she got home, she told her husband what she had done.

"How come? Was there something wrong? Were you having trouble pulling it in?" he asked, being supportive but curious.

"No. I actually pulled in first. Then I had a really weird feeling that I had to back it in. Everything was fine—we had a fantastic day, the boat ran great, and obviously it is easier to pull it straight in. I'm not sure why I did that, but I just felt like I should," Alice told him, still wondering herself.

A few days went by, and Alice and her husband decided to go out again for an afternoon boat ride. They unloaded their car of the stuff they wanted to bring on the boat and walked down to the dock. When they got there, they both noticed something looked off, but they couldn't quite put their finger on what it was. When they started to pull off the cover, they realized the boat had taken on a lot of water and was trying its best to sink. The only thing that had saved it was Alice's feeling that she had to back it in.

The leak, as it turned out, was in the boot that essentially connected the motor from the inside of the boat to the propeller on the outside. The rubber had cracked, and that piece was directly in the water. Backing in had kept the stern tied up on both sides of the boat; water was coming in, but it hadn't sunk. If Alice had pulled straight in, the entire boat would have been underwater. Following her "weird, sinking feeling" (as she put it) saved them from losing their boat, which they thought of as not only a boat, but their accessible vacation from reality.

Carla

Life just flows better when we follow our intuition. Think of it like trying to swim in a river: If you follow the natural movement of the river, it is easier; it doesn't take up too much energy because you can float along with the current. When you try swimming upstream instead, the pull of the water demands so much more from you. It takes more effort and tires you out much quicker. Essentially, going against the flow makes life harder.

Carla, a Reiki practitioner, discovered this when she was on her way to a girls retreat. She was on Interstate 84, and she had mapped out the trip on her phone. It said it would take her about two and a half hours to get to her destination. She packed her car with all the necessities for the weekend: chocolate, chips, bagels, and of course vodka. She also brought her tarot cards. She was excited and ready to go.

About a half hour into her trip, only a half hour away from home, Carla saw traffic slowing down. She noticed her GPS had changed directions and was advising her to get off at the exit coming up in about a tenth of a mile. Since she was driving in the fast lane, Carla would have had to cross traffic in order to make it; she could have, but she figured it was just construction causing the delay, so she kept going.

At the last second, Carla felt like she should take the exit. Her intuition was giving her a weird feeling. It suddenly felt like she had something clawing at her belly. She ignored it, deciding to stay the course and continue on I-84. *What will I save if I get off? Ten minutes?*

Carla thought to herself. She could spare ten minutes; it wouldn't be a big deal. So, she remained firmly in the fast lane, not even trying to move over.

Carla passed the exit. Then, all traffic stopped. She was stuck in completely immobile lanes of cars, all the drivers probably wondering, like her, what was going on. Then, Carla's GPS changed. Ahead of her, it was showing a red line, where at first it was orange. This, she knew, meant the interstate was more than just congested, it was pretty much motionless, and the arrival time was quickly getting later and later. But there was no getting off the exit now—she was too far past it already.

Carla turned off the audiobook she had been listening to and put on a local radio station to try and figure out what was happening. Nothing. Then she messaged her husband, who told her, "It looks like there was some kind of accident involving a tractor trailer."

It was a good thing she'd brought snacks. After an hour of sitting at a standstill, she opened the bag of chips meant for the weekend and said a silent apology to the girls she was meeting. Then, an hour later, she dug into the chocolate. Realizing she'd better not eat too much because who knew when she'd reach a rest stop, she restrained herself from digging into the bagels. When all was said and done, Carla sat in traffic for several hours, causing her trip to be a grand total of eight hours from start to finish.

It turned out the accident wasn't too far ahead of her, about three exits. Once traffic stopped, it took a long time for it to move again. Carla remained in almost the same spot for hours on end. Her decision to ignore her intuition cost her time. Nothing more. She was fortunate—that's not always the case.

Donna

Sometimes we are hit with life-changing moments that are, unfortunately, not by choice. These moments may encourage us to listen to our intuition. Granddaughter Crow, an award-winning author and medicine woman, shared with me: "When times get tough, it is a challenge in so many real life ways. Some of us only work with our intuition when there is not a lot at stake. But to learn how to trust our intuition when it comes to putting food on the table is a challenge. However, this is one of the best times to learn and grow."

Donna worked as a public accountant. She'd been at her job for seven years. It was a family firm: the owner was the CPA, and his wife, Claire, was the office manager. Sadly, at about the five-year mark, Donna began having a hard time dealing with Claire. Claire's daughter and son-in-law had just been hired by the firm, and Donna picked up on a weirdly competitive vibe—not from the new hires, but from Claire.

Things with Claire started to get intense. Donna knew she couldn't stay at her job, but she had rent and a car loan to pay, not to mention she had to put food on the table. In other words, Donna supported herself and couldn't afford to quit. She'd been doing a lot of intuitive studying, and she started getting a strong feeling that she had to leave, and that everything would be all right. Her clairsentience was kicking in, and although Donna was scared, she trusted it.

Donna decided to sit down with the owner. Her boss, who had no problems with her, said, "I know you're miserable, and I'm so sorry."

"I am, but I'm not going to quit," Donna insisted.

"Why?"

"Well, first of all, I'm not a quitter. Second of all, I can't leave here without having another job lined up. I have too many bills to pay," she answered, even though she knew it was going to happen.

All of a sudden, it looked like a light bulb went off over her boss's head. He said, "I get it—I will sign a pink slip so you can collect unemployment until you find a new job." He knew, just as Donna did, that her departure was inevitable, and he knew it was his wife's fault. Donna let out a sigh of relief. She was ecstatic that she'd paid attention to her intuitive impressions.

Even though Donna had no real evidence to trust her clairsentience, she had felt it would be okay, and it was. She was able to cover her bills with the unemployment income and ended up in a much better position after only a couple of months.

It can be extremely difficult to trust your intuition when you have to support yourself and you feel like trusting your intuition means you may not be able to do that. It's even more difficult when you have a family to take care of. Taking a leap of faith and trusting your gut is hard, but at times, it is extremely important to do. Working through hard times helps us grow instead of becoming stagnant.

Jess

So often we think of intuitive moments as being these huge, memorable experiences. Most of the time, they're not. They're the everyday nudges or feelings we get that we choose to follow or ignore, either consciously or unconsciously. Sometimes these everyday feelings help us at crucial moments. Sometimes they literally save lives.

Jess, an administrator at a corrections facility, tries to follow her intuition regularly. She knows how important it is. Back when she was fourteen years old, when she didn't have a care in the world, her intuition saved her from a dangerous situation.

One night, Jess had taken her dog out for a walk, as she always did. She never went far, but she did at least go around the block. It was her responsibility to make sure the dog did his business before she brought him back in. As she was walking, she saw a man standing about twenty-five yards away. There was nothing extraordinary about him; he looked pretty average and nonthreatening, as far as her fourteen-year-old self could see.

But something—something important—told Jess the man was dangerous. Goosebumps were rising on her entire body. (Jess now recognizes this as a telltale sign of her intuitive awareness.) So, Jess picked up her dog and ran as fast as she could. When she looked back, Jess saw the man running toward her.

Jess began to sprint, digging deep for extra power, and mercifully, she made it to her house. Once inside, she peeked out the window and saw the man had turned tail and was running away, glancing over his shoulder as he went. Thankfully, Jess had made it home before the man could catch her. She was completely freaked out, but extremely happy she trusted the bad vibes she had picked up on.

· · · · · **—** · · · · ·

PONDER THIS
TRUST THE VIBES

Pay attention when you feel someone is giving off negative energy. Trust your vibes! But, when assessing a person's negative vibes, make sure to ask yourself:

Is it because you don't like the person?

Is it because they are not trustworthy?

Is it because they don't like you?

Is it because they have their own issues, which have nothing to do with the matter at hand?

Is it because they are lying to you?

After each question, pay attention to what you're feeling. Are you feeling sludge oozing from them? Or are things feeling light and airy? Determining why you feel the way you do can help you move forward and can even help enhance your interpretations of your intuitive gifts.

Our body has a way of telling us something when our mind is having a hard time understanding what our soul is trying to share. Goosebumps, though sometimes just a reaction to a cold temperature, routinely pop up to alert us our intuition is trying to get our attention. You may get them on your arms, or your head, or all over your body. Pay attention to other intuitive indications that appear in addition to the goosebumps to better guide you.

Ben

Clairsentience doesn't care whether you are a cop or a college student. When you don't listen to your intuition, there's usually some kind of detrimental effect, even if it's not life-and-death.

Ben was a police officer in New York. He normally walked a beat, and that basically involved keeping abreast of a twenty-square-block radius. He and the other police officers made an hourly check in from a call box. He would share what he'd seen, what he'd done, if there were any issues or things that needed following up, etc. Mostly, this task was just to let police headquarters know he was safe and continuing to walk his post.

One beautiful fall day, Ben was told to stand by. Headquarters stated a car was heading out and was going to be picking him up. Ben was near the end of his shift, so they were going to bring him in to write up all his reports for the day. That was the norm, the usual procedure, the customary routine for every work shift, and it had never been an issue for Ben.

Today, it was an issue. He started getting a really bad feeling. Ben couldn't put his finger on it, but he felt like something bad was going to happen. He told headquarters he had a hunch that he should stay out and walk his area again, but they told him no, he was to get in the car. Ben was pretty new to the job, and being a solo officer meant that he was all alone; he knew he had no backup if something was going down, so he didn't push too hard against authority.

Ben went to headquarters and worked on his reports. Nothing much had happened during his shift, so there wasn't a whole lot of work to be done. The entire time he was typing up his reports, he continued to have a nagging feeling that something was wrong. Like most cops, Ben had been told by his training officer, "Don't ever ignore your gut. Pay attention to the hunches you have. One day they may just save your life!" So, Ben went to his supervisor.

"Sir, I don't know what's happening, but I feel like something is about to pop off," he explained.

"Well, there's always something, now isn't there?" his boss responded.

"I know, but this feels different. I'm telling you I have a bad feeling inside. My gut is telling me there's something wrong."

"I get it—but unless you have something a bit more concrete to go on, you should just finish up your reports. Don't you want to get home to your wife?" his supervisor asked, blowing him off in a nice way.

Although he still had a feeling that something was amiss, Ben let it go. After all, it wasn't anything tangible, just his own sensations making the hair on his arms stand up. So, he gave in and decided he would just go home when he was done.

As Ben was finishing up his reports, he heard a call come through on the radio. This particular broadcast sparked his interest because it was at the same intersection he made his check-in calls from. He stopped what he was doing and listened intently to what the dispatcher had just said.

"Armed robbery in progress," he heard, and a store at that location was named.

Ben grabbed the driver that had brought him into the station, told his supervisor what he'd just heard, and headed back to where he had just been picked up. Unfortunately, his cop's hunch had been right on. Something bad had indeed happened: the owner of the shop immediately next to the call box had been shot and killed during the armed robbery.

It's important to note that Ben didn't just have a hunch about himself—he was sensitive to others as well. Though Ben isn't positive what the outcome would have been had he stayed, he undeniably knew there was trouble in the air, and it turned out to be life-and-death.

Madison

Madison had a similar feeling at a college party. She had been recruited by her college to play lacrosse. She loved the game and her teammates; she fit right in and enjoyed hanging out with them. She jokes that they were like the same people, all having the same interests.

One night, Madison was in a teammate's dorm room. Her and her friends were partying, drinking, dancing, and generally having a great time. They weren't planning on going out—it was only Tuesday, after all. They were, however, letting off some steam from a long, tough practice that afternoon.

Madison went to the bathroom and got a really weird feeling. She'd overdone it before, so she was familiar with what it felt like to throw up everything she'd eaten that day—but that wasn't what this was. She felt sick, but not from the alcohol. Her stomach was not doing so well.

She told her roommate, Sam, that they needed to leave right away.

Her friend just laughed and said, "No way! I'm having too much fun!"

"Sam, I'm telling you we have to go, now!" Madison reiterated, but Sam just thought she was being a buzzkill, so she said goodbye to her.

Madison went back to her dorm room, not sure what was going on. She worried that perhaps it was just her fear of getting in trouble, but at the same time, she felt very strongly that she'd repeatedly gotten the message to leave. She was about to call her mom to check in back home when she heard a commotion in the hallway: breaking glass and people yelling. Madison cracked the door and peeked out, and what she saw confirmed her feeling that trouble had been brewing.

The Resident Attendant was standing in the hallway with her teammates. They had been trying to hide the fact that they were drinking, and in the process, they dropped and broke a few bottles. Madison's teammates all got in trouble—and it was worse than just being yelled at. They were all suspended from school for a week, and they were also suspended from lacrosse games and practice for the same time period.

Trying to distinguish between fear and intuition is probably one of the most difficult tasks we face when tuning in. Fear habitually drives our inability to trust our instincts with confidence, as it makes us worry about an outcome and whether we are right or wrong. While we all make some decisions based on fear, when you continually feel the same impression over and over again, it's more important to be steadfast in trusting your soul's intuitive wisdom.

· · · · · · — · · · · · ·

PONDER THIS
FEAR OR INTUITION?

One way to determine if you are feeling fear or intuition is to ground yourself. First, think of a situation where you are having a hard time discerning whether fear or intuition is guiding you. Then, close your eyes and imagine you have tree roots coming out of the bottoms of your feet, reaching all the way down into the center of the earth. Allow your feet to feel warm, and let that warmth spread up through your body. Stay still for as long as you need to in order to feel that connection.

Once you feel relaxed, think of the situation again. Are you able to remain peaceful? Or do you feel jumpy, distracted, or nervous? If you're still peaceful, you are experiencing an intuitive reaction, regardless of what the situation is. If not, then it's most likely your fear getting in the way of your intuitive guidance system.

So often I'm asked how to know if the clairsentient vibe a person is feeling is real or not. After all, if you followed the feeling you had and nothing went wrong, who's to say something bad would have happened if you hadn't? That is the question, and it's one I'm quite content to not find out the answer to. We know from experience what happens when we swim upstream—it makes everything more difficult. Is it worth the aggravation? Instead, learn to trust your gut.

Carrie

Childhood is supposed to be a time of joy, but so many children are faced with stressful and even downright disturbing situations. Often, these situations create the perfect setting for metaphysical encounters. In fact, these unpleasant episodes are frequently the catalysts that open up intuitive awareness.

Such was the case for Carrie. When she was a child, she endured abuse by a close family member. He threatened that if she told anyone what was going on, it would wreak havoc on her family, and that no one would believe her anyway. Believing she had no one to turn to, she kept the abuse a secret—for a little while, anyway.

Over time, Carrie developed a sixth sense. She counted on this sense to warn her when danger was coming. Sometimes she was able to circumvent the abuse, but not always. One thing she held on to throughout that dark time in her life was knowing that it would end. She also felt that she would be okay—she felt it all the way down to her bones.

Eventually, Carrie exposed her abuser. Her intuition had continually expressed to her that she would be okay. And, thankfully, she is. She knows, to this day, that without her intuition assuring her that she would make it through, she may not have.

Let's talk about trusting our intuition even when we don't know why we are experiencing a clairsentient feeling. Every moment of every day, we have choices to make; usually, these choices are not life-altering, but some can be. Most of the time, the outcome of the decision we make will be evident sooner or later. When you trust your intuitive guidance system, there is a better chance that the outcome will be positive instead of negative. Always trust your gut instinct, no matter how your intuitive nudges show up.

Beth

Beth was an advertising executive. She was busy, but she always made time for her family. One beautiful Saturday morning, Beth was getting ready to visit her brother and sister-in-law and their young kids; she planned to stop and pick up her mother along the way. Beth was really looking forward to the ride with her mom, and to catching up with her nieces. The sun was shining, and the forecast called for nice weather to continue all weekend. It was going to be the perfect trip.

Beth finished putting on her makeup, then packed some drinks for the three-hour drive. All was as it should have been. Suddenly, just as Beth was about to head out, she got a really bad feeling. She had a strong intuitive feeling to stay home. She kept feeling like something was directing her: "Don't go! Just don't do it."

Beth called her mom and told her how she felt.

"What the heck are you talking about? Why would you say that?" her mother responded.

"I don't know. I just feel like it's not a good idea, at all. I feel really strongly about it. And I can't tell you why. I just finished getting ready and was actually really excited to go, but something just feels wrong … I can feel it from the top of my head to the tips of my toes," Beth continued, trying to explain how she felt.

"That makes no sense. Should we take a different route or something? Do you want to leave a bit later? Do you need to run and have your car checked out quickly before we go?"

Beth thought about everything her mom had suggested. The bottom line, she realized, was that her mind was made up.

"Mom, I don't know. I just have an incredibly strong feeling that we can't go. Something doesn't feel right. I can't put my finger on what it is, but I feel it deep down to the bottom of my soul. I can't explain it other than that. I just feel like our lives will never be the same if we go, and not in a good way. In a very, very bad way."

Beth called her brother and apologized for changing their plans, but they took it very well. They made a plan to try again the following week and ended up having a great visit.

When I asked Beth if she ever figured out if something had occurred, like a bad accident along their route or a serious illness or something, she answered, "No. Nothing that I could pinpoint. I still can't fathom why I had such an intense feeling."

As far as Beth could remember, this was the first time she had ever acted on her intuition. It was also the first time she'd received such an incredibly confusing message. To this day, she still strongly believes that if she hadn't followed her intuition, she may not be here.

Clairsentience can materialize as a gut feeling or another sensation in the body. The impressions that physically affect the body are trying to help us in some way. With a bit of practice, we can learn to tune in to these clairsentient abilities even more.

EXERCISE Trust Your Body

When you have an intuitive feeling and are unsure of what it means or whether you should follow it, you can ask for validation.

Use your body as a type of pendulum and see which way you sway. Start by creating two different responses: positive and negative. Think of something that makes you feel overwhelmingly positive and note how your body responds as you're thinking of it. Pay attention to whether you feel pulled in one direction. Next, think of something absolutely negative. Again, note how your body feels and if you're being pulled in a certain direction.

Then, ask the question you want validated. Pay attention to which direction your body intuitively leans. And, as always, if you're not sure of the answer, ask for validation again.

Samantha, Emma, and Mia

Cemeteries are always spookier in the dark. Teenagers often find themselves drawn to cemeteries: the aura surrounding them, the thrill of possibility … It can be fun to scare ourselves silly, with nothing needed other than a headstone or two to conjure up images of ghosts and thoughts of the dead reaching out from beyond the grave. Visiting cemeteries at night is a popular pastime for many a teen, and to be honest, many an adult as well!

One autumn night, when the moon was barely a sliver, Samantha, Emma, and Mia decided to have some fun. The girls were just driving around, and they decided they would stop at the next cemetery they came across. They wanted to be scared—fright in a fun way was their goal. They were totally open to the possibility of dead people showing up, though they knew chances were slim that they'd experience a full apparition.

The girls pulled up to an old, dark, creepy-looking cemetery in the town of Monroe, Connecticut, about twenty minutes from Samantha's hometown. It felt like the perfect place to lose their composure for a little bit, so they got out of their car and walked into the graveyard. They wandered around, scaring one another randomly. It was a spooky setting, so shouting a mere "Boo!" was working.

Eventually, the girls decided they wanted to let themselves be guided to something extraordinary, though they didn't know what it would be. They agreed to go wherever they felt intuitively pulled. The girls split up and began hunting for ghosts in different areas in the cemetery. Suddenly, at the same time, they all began heading toward one area of the cemetery. They looked at each other, bewildered, wondering what was drawing them, as they continued walking, the distance to one another closing.

By the time the girls were standing side-by-side, they were covered in goosebumps. They looked at the grave directly in front of them—where Ed and Lorraine Warren were buried. The girls had no idea that this cemetery was the final resting site of two of the most famous ghost hunters in the country! This excited them so much that they sat right down and remained silent for a moment, reverently tuning in to the energy that had brought them there. They felt welcomed. In that moment, they knew they had experienced a feeling unlike any other—not only were they connected to each other, they were also connected to the famous duo! This experience created an even greater kinship between Samantha, Emma, and Mia. The night was a success.

While the girls aren't sure if it was actually the Warrens' spirits calling them over or just their intuition drawing them to the deceased couple, it was still an amazing experience, one not to be forgotten anytime soon. As I said before, metaphysical experiences don't always need to be named—the psychic senses that guide you aren't worried about whether you know what gift you're using. It is more important to recognize that your intuition is present.

Genevieve

Genevieve was a student at UCSC and had just finished the quarter. She was excited because her and her roommates had a long break, and they were going to take advantage of it. It was party time! Genevieve and her roommates had always gotten along great. That's why, when it came time to renew their lease, Genevieve was surprised she decided not to.

Genevieve didn't know why, but she had the strangest feeling that she needed to move on. It felt like the home she'd been sharing for the past year was no longer where she was supposed to live—it wasn't supposed to be her house anymore. She'd had no problems with the other students she shared the place with—no issues with her roommates at all! She just felt it would be better for her if she looked for a different house, with different roommates.

When Genevieve told her roommates she was not renewing her lease, they asked if there was a specific reason she was leaving.

She insisted she just had a feeling she needed to follow a different path. That path led her to a new house with new roommates. They immediately hit it off. In fact, she became best friends with some of them almost from the moment she moved in! That, in turn, started a snowball effect: her new roommates exposed her to other great people, which increased her social network even more, and her friend group exponentially expanded. And in the process of making new friends, Genevieve tried a lot of previously unexplored activities, several of which she loved—she even went on to become a DJ! She's so happy she followed her gut instincts.

Genevieve's story is not uncommon. Actually, this sort of thing is a widespread phenomenon. Genevieve got the feeling that she was supposed to move on, even though she lived with great people in a perfectly fine place. The only difference between Genevieve and someone else is that she trusted that feeling. In doing so, she took a big chance. She trusted that her intuition—her clairsentience—was nudging her to do something that would make her life better in some way. She believed that her soul had her best interests in mind and had confidence in her ability to discern what it was telling her.

Carol

Carol, a college professor, also believed in the pull of her soul. She'd always had a lifelong fascination with Ireland; she loved the movies, music, dancing, and everything else related to a real Irish life. She'd grown up feeling a strong Celtic connection: a longing, almost a familiarity, attached to the country of Ireland, though she'd never been there.

Carol did some research but found she had no Irish relatives. She discovered there was absolutely no Irish connection in the family at all! But still, she felt so drawn to it. Carol decided to ask her mother who, again, confirmed the family wasn't Irish. So, she let it go.

A few weeks later, Carol once again found herself wondering about her connection to Ireland. She decided to do DNA testing. The results she received had her confused—her DNA showed she was half British and half Irish. Carol's mother insisted she had no idea how that was possible. So, Carol ordered DNA tests for both of her parents, and it turned out her dad was almost totally British, with a negligent amount of Irish DNA, and her mom had no Irish DNA at all. But Carol knew there had to be something more going on for her to be 50 percent Irish. She decided to reach out to her friend who was a geneticist.

"Is there any way that I could have 50 percent Irish DNA when only my father has a smidge of Irish DNA?" she asked.

"Well, no. For you to have that much of your ancestry from Ireland, you'd need to have at least one of your parents come from Irish descent," her friend explained.

By this point, time had passed and there were new test sites where anyone could do DNA testing that showed their ancestry. Carol decided to go on one of these sites. When her test results came back, they were basically the same. The website also directed her to various other people who shared the same DNA, numerous relatives she hadn't known she had.

Carol was confused by these results, so she went ahead and tried another DNA testing site, which showed the same results for a third time. This time, Carol went to her mother and asked if she knew any of the other listed relatives. Her mother answered with the same definitive "No."

The tests also showed Carol's relation to her parent's DNA— her mother's DNA showed a 100 percent relation, but her father's

DNA was only 1.5 percent related to her own. With her mother still denying having any knowledge about the situation, Carol called her geneticist friend once more.

"Any chance this is in error? Should I question the paternity?"

"No chance at this point. Too many tests have been run. Yes, you definitely need to question paternity," she responded. "There is a relative connection, but there is no way he is your father."

Carol found out her parents were actually second cousins. They'd gotten married a long time ago, and it was common back then. She wondered if that was why the DNA came back strange. But after her friend emphatically told her in no uncertain terms that the man she'd called Dad since birth was not her actual father, she knew that she needed to question her mom again.

Finally, Carol invited her mom to lunch. Carol asked if her parents had ever used fertility treatments. After denying everything once again, her mother paled. She told Carol she knew what was happening—she knew the reason he wasn't showing up as her biological father—and she hadn't put it together until that moment. She shared with Carol that they had separated for a couple of months before Carol was born. In that time, Carol's mother had fallen for someone much older than herself, someone she worked with. She never considered the possibility that she could conceive with him because of his age. They were together for a very short time before she went back to Carol's dad.

Her mom also told her that one of the reasons they had initially split was because they had been trying to have kids for a long time but never had any success. It had put a lot of pressure on their relationship and caused a lot of stress. After they got back together, a month or so later, Carol's mother discovered she was pregnant. When they went to the doctor, they were told they may have been successful this time because they hadn't had sex in a while, and it could have helped the process along. They never thought twice about it, and they never successfully got pregnant again.

Carol discovered that her Irish roots were real. Her biological father, long passed by then, was 100 percent Irish. She understood now why her intuition was drawing her to Ireland. For Carol, this was validation she needed, and although it challenged everything she'd grown up knowing to be true, it was a relief to know why she'd had such strong feelings.

Clairempathy

Clairempathy is similar to clairsentience in that it's an intuitive feeling you get, but it is more about feeling what others feel as opposed to feeling your own intuitive guidance system. Think of it like this: if you are with someone who is severely depressed or even manically happy and then you start feeling like that for no reason, you're probably empathic, or you're using clairempathy to feel what they feel. This can happen with negative or positive emotions, or even when there is something wrong with someone, such as illness or an altered mental state.

Doreen

Kids are very susceptible to clairempathic gifts. Sometimes it's due to learning to protect themselves. Mercifully, though, not everyone reaches their intuitive breakthrough moment because of childhood trauma. Sometimes children discover their gifts because they are frequently alone. It can sort of become a game for them. Those kids may be very creative or regularly interact with imaginary playmates.

In Doreen's case, she started experiencing clairempathy in the 1950s. Doreen was an only child. She longed for siblings to play with. Some of you reading this may have craved respite from your brother or sister, but not Doreen. She yearned for company.

Doreen's mother was always busy. As she put it, she was the "typical fifties housewife": cleaning and cooking and making the home comfortable for when Doreen's father came home. This left Doreen to play by herself for many hours a day. She often fantasized about playdates joining her for tea parties or to play with her dolls; she swore that she could feel what her imaginary playmates were feeling. Over time, Doreen noticed she could feel the mood her mother was in when she was cooking. And she even went so far as to feel the mood her dad was in when he got home from work.

Luckily, there were no traumatic or abusive events that caused the awakening of Doreen's clairempathy. Instead, it was loneliness that cultivated her intuition. Looking back, she is happy she had the time alone. She believes her clairempathy is a great gift, and she's been able to carry it into adulthood.

Mattias

Clairempathic and clairsentient gifts can be used to assist others in many ways. Mattias found that out while working in healthcare. As part of his job, he had to talk to patients regarding their bills. He also helped them find and receive the services they needed.

At first, when he started working in this position, he was just kind of "doing his job." But after a bit of time, he realized he was beginning to feel their emotions and feelings. He knew, even if the patient told him everything was okay, when they weren't telling him the truth. Mattias discovered that when he allowed himself to open his awareness, he was able to use his empathic abilities to feel what patients were going through.

Mattias also realized that using his gifts was enhancing his ability to make better decisions and choices for patients. And, more importantly, he was able to get them the services they needed, even when they didn't tell him directly. Mattias developed an appreciation for his clairempathic gifts.

With time, Mattias noticed if he was having a bad day and didn't tune in to patients, it was inevitable that they would both hang up the phone miserable. In order to combat that, he started each shift with a silent meditation, which he soon understood helped him achieve a greater connection. It also improved his mood, and he was able to bring that happiness home to his family.

EXERCISE Clairempathy

When we experience clairempathy, it can be hard to understand. If you're unsure about whether a feeling is coming from you or someone else, try this simple exercise.

Stand with your feet firmly planted. Then allow yourself to feel. Trust your intuition. If the alert is for you, you may feel your feet rooted to the ground; feel connected to the earth for just a moment. If the feeling is coming from someone else, instead of feeling fixed to the ground, it may feel as though you are floating or even flying toward someone— your clairempathy may be enlightening you about the person who is feeling this way.

Though this exercise may not answer all of your questions, it can be a great starting point to determine if a feeling is yours or not.

Feel It

As we grow, we discover our sixth sense really does exist. I believe clairsentience should actually be called our first sense because it is vital to our survival. Clairsentience is perhaps the strongest of these metaphysical senses, and the more you welcome it, the more you will come to value it.

Clairempathy may not be as easy to recognize in the beginning, but discerning whether you're feeling someone else's emotions becomes easier with practice. Eventually, others' emotions will feel foreign and even sudden.

You, and only you, can uncover just how much having clear intuitive feelings can help you in life. If—and it's a big if—you use them.

PRO TIP

Those feelings in your body—they may be your intuition. And sometimes, the emotions you feel may not be yours.

Chapter 3
CLAIRCOGNIZANCE

Have you ever known something that you should have no way of knowing? It can be difficult to trust this inner wisdom. However, if you know it, you know it. There's usually a reason you know it; either you've experienced it, you've held it, you've lived through it, you've seen it for yourself, or you have other information that allows you to know something without any doubt. But how do you trust that your knowledge is real when you have no proof? That's claircognizance: knowing something to be true, even when you have no external, tangible evidence to support what you know. You just know!

Listening to Inner Wisdom

Claircognizance, a clear knowing, will frequently be accompanied by clairsentience, a clear feeling. Alternatively, it can present as an impression that you receive unexpectedly.

Awyn Dawn

Awyn Dawn, the award-winning author of *Paganism on Parole*, shares her incredible journey of discovering her intuition. Though she doubted her intuition along the way, she just knew she needed to make a huge life change:

> There is always fear when you step into a new life. This past year, my intuition—or rather, my ability to trust it—was put to the test. Moving to England from the United States was a dream of mine. But when I hit a hiccup early on, I had to decide: give up, or trust my instinct and keep going. I knew it was meant to be, so I persevered.
>
> It took a year of work. A year of paying off debts and selling almost everything I owned. It took a lot of leaps of faith, but I knew I had to move forward. Because I have a felonious background, there was a chance that my visa application would get denied. But I went through the motions anyway because my intuition told me that this was the future for me.
>
> After a long twelve months and thousands of dollars invested, my visa application got approved. It was a moment of relief that reaffirmed that my intuition never leads me astray.
>
> —Awyn Dawn

If Awyn hadn't believed her intuitive knowledge, she never would have made it to England. I, personally, am glad she did because the pictures she posts are amazing! More importantly, I can see that she is living her best life. Although there was no promise of certainty, Awyn still followed her instincts, and it paid off. As with every intuitive ability, we have a choice: we can ignore our instincts, or we can pay attention to them and trust they're guiding us to something better.

Amy

Amy, a public health worker who worked in emergency preparedness and communicable disease investigation, shared with me that she uses her intuition at work all the time. It helps her feel which direction she should go in her investigations. But Amy also told me that one of the most powerful intuitive episodes she had didn't have anything to do with her work—it was about her son, who was away at college.

Amy had been in the middle of putting groceries away. She stopped dead in her tracks, almost dropping a full container of fruit. She knew something was wrong. She knew with complete certainty! She just wasn't sure what it was.

It was her son's freshman year of college. He was adapting quite well and making friends. He'd even made the football team and was doing well academically. Still, out of nowhere, Amy knew something bad was happening to him. It wasn't just a feeling—she *knew*. Amy called him and asked what was happening, trying to be casual so as not to freak him out. He told her everything was fine; he was just getting back from practice and said he was excited about the team.

Amy was happy he was doing well, so she didn't push too hard. After she hung up, however, her knowledge that something really bad was brewing hadn't gone away. So, Amy called her son again. This time it went to his voicemail, and she knew it was imperative she talk to him because the knowing she was experiencing was getting stronger. She continued calling him. It was almost as though with each call, she knew whatever was happening was becoming more significant. She felt danger and consequence.

With each call that went unanswered, Amy's concern grew. That was it—she would call his RA if he didn't answer. She dialed his number one more time, and he finally answered.

"Mom, what?!?" he shouted.

"Calm down! What is happening?" she asked. "What is going on? I know it's something bad!"

"Mom! My dorm got broken into and we were robbed! I want my damn stuff back, now!" he yelled, presumably to the kid who'd stolen his stuff.

She heard some mumbling in the background.

"Hey, stay with me. Tell him you're going to the RA if he doesn't return it right now," she told him in a quieter voice.

Her son had gone to confront the thief and get his things back, and it was evident the conversation had become very emotionally heated, with significant potential to escalate. Amy made him stay on the phone with her and was able to calm him down.

After this event, Amy's son started paying attention to her intuition, and he is even developing his own relationship with his soul senses.

Most parents will tell you it's uncanny the way they just know when there is something bad happening to their kids. There is a significant connection between a parent and a child, and it increases their sensitivity. I know it's happened to me plenty of times—so much so that my kids joke they can never get away with anything because "Mom always knows!" This intuitive knowing also happens with twins and even spouses at times; they report the ability to finish each other's sentences or to pick up the phone and call the other person exactly when something important is happening.

Jim

When it comes to their kids, a parent's intuition tends to go into overdrive. This happened when Jim was getting ready to go on a drive with his family. They were all in the car, ready to go, but Jim didn't move.

"Jim?" his wife said questioningly.

He just sat there.

"Dad?" one of their kids said after he still hadn't moved.

He sat there, still.

Out of nowhere, a carload full of young kids flew by their driveway; they must have been going about ninety miles per hour. Not only would the vehicle have hit them, but Jim's family and the teens driving the other car would probably all have been killed. Everyone in the car with Jim stared at him in shock. He doesn't know how, but he just knew to stay put.

This type of claircognizance is not all that unusual. Many people attribute it to their guardian angel. I believe this can be the work of your guides, or a result of your soul's connection to your guides, the angels, and the universe, who are letting you know it's not time for you to leave this world yet.

Ash

Ash, a student at the time, shared a similar experience: "One night I was driving, headed home after a long day. I stopped at a red light. When the light turned green, my intuition told me not to go. A few seconds later, a large truck ran their red light, speeding through the intersection. They would have smashed right into my car if I had gone when the light turned green." She calls this experience her "red light, green light" intuition. Somehow, Ash knew to stay still, not move, do nothing. It wasn't something she necessarily felt coming into the intersection. Rather, it was a last-minute warning—a highly charged, do-or-die moment. Ash's full, unwavering belief that her intuition was warning her kept her safe.

Erin

A parent's connection to their child often leads to claircognizance, as Erin was to discover. Erin's daughter, Brielle, began having seizures at a young age. After the first one occurred, Erin brought her to her pediatrician immediately. The pediatrician believed Brielle had hit her head or something; there were no concrete or definitive answers. So, Brielle was sent home, and Erin was told to keep an eye on her.

Erin knew her daughter would have another seizure. She didn't know how she knew, but she knew. She told Brielle's doctor, to no avail.

It happened again, another seizure, as Erin knew it would. She bypassed the pediatrician and went straight to the emergency room, where they did some tests that had inconclusive results. After a few days in the hospital with no further seizures, the ER doctor told Erin to bring Brielle home; she would be okay now. Erin knew he was wrong, but having no proof, she had to acquiesce.

They were home for one night. The next evening, Erin knew her daughter was going to have another seizure. She had no evidence, no reason to believe it, but she knew. It was imperative that she respond rapidly, with her full attention. So, Erin called her brother and asked him to come watch Brielle's younger sister even though nothing had happened yet. Right after Erin's brother arrived to babysit, Erin had to rush Brielle to the hospital—she had begun seizing yet again.

The doctor there told her they weren't sure what was happening but prescribed anti-seizure procedures. Erin had to bring Brielle in every month for treatment. Years later, Brielle was still having regular seizures. The treatments did not fully prevent them, and on top of that, the treatments made her lethargic. Erin talked to the doctor about changing Brielle's diet further; she'd already switched to mostly healthy foods, but she suggested cutting out all sugars, white flour products, etc. The doctor told Erin that had nothing to do with it and he'd see them the next month for another treatment.

However, in her heart, Erin just knew what she needed to do for her daughter. She cut out all sugars and white flour. She fed her only homemade meals so she could monitor the sugar and flour intake. And, with time, her daughter improved. Although the doctor never agreed that this dietary change was what stopped the seizures, he agreed that Brielle no longer needed the other treatments. Erin knew, though, and she continued that diet for her daughter until her adolescence. No more seizures.

· · · · · · — · · · · · ·
PONDER THIS
CLAIRCOGNIZANT WARNINGS

A claircognizant warning is important! This is different from regular claircognizance. Consider the following if you are unsure whether you should follow the guidance you've instantly been given:

+ Is it dangerous? Do you need to heed the warning immediately?
+ If you don't heed the warning, will it be detrimental to you in some way?

If you answer yes to either of those questions in the split second after your soul is trying to help you, then the answer is clear: heed the warning! You're better off following your claircognizant warning; you can think about what the outcome may have been if you hadn't listened to your claircognizance after the fact.

As you've no doubt realized by now, some, but not all, intuitive guidance is critical. With claircognizance, if it is imperative that you respect your soul's message, you'll know. A strong knowing will show up in your life in a variety of ways. Again, claircognizance is not always life-and-death, but that doesn't mean it's not important.

Ruby

A parent's intuition works whether you're in the same house or hundreds of miles away from your kid—physical distance makes no difference. Ruby figured that out when her son, Stan, was living in an apartment six hours away.

Stan had begun a new career and was working a lot. Even though he was really busy, he'd been doing pretty good. One day, he called his mom and told her he was worn down and had a cold. He said he was still going to work every day even though he was totally exhausted. Immediately, Ruby knew this wasn't a regular cold.

"You need to get a COVID test right away," Ruby told him.

He said, "No way; I've had COVID. This is not COVID. It's just a cold, Mom. No big deal."

But Ruby knew. Without even seeing him, she knew. She did not let up. "Look, Stan. I know it's COVID. Just humor me and listen to your mother."

So, he put his mask on and ran to the drugstore to buy a test. An hour later, he called his mother and told her she was right: it was COVID. Since COVID is highly contagious and can be life-threatening, Stan knew this was not something to mess around with. Testing positive allowed Stan to take off the time he needed to rest and get better, rather than pushing through and making his bout with the virus worse. Even though Stan hadn't believed his mother at first, he was glad he'd called her.

Nancy

Nancy was a world traveler. She was used to living in foreign countries, as she had grown up overseas. When she was living in the

States, it seemed her family never stayed in one place for long. She was used to moving around and felt it was a positive experience.

However, when Nancy's daughter wanted to spend her collegiate years overseas in Japan, Nancy and her husband hesitated. Nancy knew how valuable it was to experience other places and cultures, but she also knew it would be hard having her daughter on the other side of the world. Nancy and her husband debated whether it was worth spending the money and having her so far away. But all the while, Nancy knew in her soul that her daughter was going to be okay, and that she needed this experience for her independence. Ultimately, Nancy knew that she had to support her daughter's endeavors.

Her daughter ended up going to school overseas for film production. Nancy and her husband supported their daughter throughout her years there. At the same time Nancy's claircognizance told her that her daughter was okay in Japan, it was also telling her that her daughter was not going to work in the field she'd studied after she graduated. Nancy explained to her husband that she knew, deep down, that when their daughter came home after graduation, she would go in a totally different direction—holistic healing. Sure enough, Nancy's daughter is actively pursuing that direction now. She's already receiving training in Reiki and is loving it!

As Nancy's story shows, just because we know something intuitively doesn't mean we have to change the trajectory of the events. Sometimes, it means we have to believe that even if a situation is not going to have the desired outcome (or even the expected outcome), it's still all right and often beneficial to let things run their course.

Jennifer

Parenting doesn't come with a guide, so we have to trust our intuition on so many levels. We constantly make decisions that affect our children's lives as well as our own. These everyday choices add up:

trying to do the right thing, allowing them to go to a party, feeling out their friends, knowing what school may be right for them, finding them doctors … Parents are always wondering if we are doing right by our children.

Among the many challenges she faced as a mom, Jennifer had to make a crucial decision when it came to her son, Nathan. When Nathan was five years old, he got really sick. Jennifer started off treating him at home, but it didn't seem to be working. He was getting worse. His fever continued rising, and her intuition told her she couldn't wait—she needed to take him to the emergency room. Once there, the ER staff confirmed she had made the right decision. They told her the doctor that would be treating Nathan would be there shortly.

Jennifer's heart was pounding. She was worried, and rightly so! Her son had continued to decline. When the doctor came in, she instantly didn't like him. He was rude and had no bedside manner. He didn't try to make her feel better; in fact, he ignored her. She was not pleased with the doctor—until something happened to change her mind.

The doctor turned to Jennifer and told her he had been trained to handle this type of situation. However, he was going to go against what he'd been taught. When she asked why, he answered that he just knew he needed to go with his instincts rather than follow the normal protocol. She looked at him and decided right then and there she needed to trust him. So, she did. She knew, because her intuition confirmed it, that he was doing the right thing.

The doctor went on to prescribe medicine, explaining that he had been a doctor for decades, but he was trying something different because he knew it was right for Nathan. Once again, Jennifer's gut told her to trust him. Within twenty-four hours, her son was all better. Everyone at the hospital was shocked. They hadn't expected him to be ready to go home, let alone be rid of the fever that was escalating the night before.

We are taught to trust the professionals, but if you have children, you know as well as I do that parents don't usually just blindly listen to them. And if we do, it's because we either have absolutely no idea what else to do, or we've been indoctrinated in some way to think our opinions don't matter. Jennifer knew deep down that, although she felt an initial dislike, she had to let the doctor do his job, and thankfully, the doctor trusted his intuition. We should always check in with our gut to make sure something feels right or true.

A similar thing happened to me when I was driving my baby to the doctor years ago. The appointment was to decide whether or not she needed to have surgery on her ears to put in tubes that would help her ears drain properly. The doctor was insistent that she needed to have the surgery, but I knew in my gut that it wasn't right. I knew, intuitively, that my baby needed to stop eating dairy. I asked for a sign to confirm my knowing (we'll talk more about this in chapter 7), and sure enough, I immediately got one. The car in front of me had a bumper sticker on it that said "Trust Your Angels." At the time, I was teaching courses about learning how to trust the messages you receive from your guides and angels. My message couldn't have been any clearer. And, more importantly, for us, it was the right decision. Following my intuition to cut out dairy healed my daughter's ears. This is by no means an instruction to ignore your physician's advice—it is merely an example of turning to your intuitive guidance system for validation.

Matthew

Children are one of the greatest joys in life, and yes, I speak from experience. I'm not saying parenthood is easy, but the reality is most of us wouldn't trade our children for the world. That's why it can be so difficult when we lose one, even before they are born.

Matthew was at work one day when, for no reason at all, he instantly knew his wife was pregnant. It was like a light bulb went off. It wasn't like he and his wife were necessarily trying to conceive; they weren't. But they also weren't *not* trying. However, his wife hadn't said anything at all about possibly being pregnant.

Still, Matthew couldn't shake the feeling. He called his wife and told her, "You're pregnant."

It wasn't a question. It was a statement. She paused, not understanding what he was talking about.

"No, I'm not," she answered. However, that night, she took a pregnancy test. It was positive.

"I don't know how you knew, but you were right! I'm pregnant!" she exclaimed.

Matthew, seeing her face, felt terrible—he was not excited at all. She was beyond happy, but what he had to tell her next would crush her.

"I'm sorry, honey. I want to be excited, but I just can't," he said.

His wife didn't understand. She knew they hadn't been intentionally trying to get pregnant, but he didn't *not* want to have a baby, right? She asked him what was going on.

"Of course I do! I just have a bad feeling that something's going to happen. In fact, I'm sure of it. I'm sorry! But it's okay, because we will have others," he told her, sure of his words, if not his delivery.

That night, his wife started feeling pain in her abdominal area. It went away, but the next day it returned. It was excruciating. She was in so much pain; she didn't know what was happening. But Matthew did. This was it. He knew they were losing the baby.

They went to the doctor first thing the next morning. Unfortunately, he'd been right. He knew something would be wrong, and sure enough, it was. The doctor told them the reason she was in so much distress was because it was an ectopic pregnancy, and she would not have been able to carry the baby to term. They lost the baby; it had never been a viable embryo. But Matthew's claircognizance almost certainly helped them both get through it. And, soon after, they ended up having several healthy children with no issues at all.

Grace

Grace also experienced claircognizance about pregnancy. She had an excruciating pain in her abdominal area and had no idea what it was. At one point, it got so bad that she passed out, and her husband called the ambulance. She had to have emergency surgery to have one of her ovaries removed. Unbeknownst to Grace, she'd been pregnant, but it wasn't a viable pregnancy, and it almost killed her.

After her surgery, Grace's doctor cautioned that conceiving a child in the future would probably be difficult; it would be hard to get pregnant, and she may not be able to sustain a pregnancy. But Grace left the hospital knowing that she would someday have a baby and it would be fine—both the baby and the pregnancy. Her intuition was right! Her baby boy is now twenty-three years old.

Blossom

Family connections are vital for so many reasons. Blossom was close to her family even though they didn't live near each other anymore. One day, she had an epiphany that she had to go see her dad. Unfortunately, she went to college in California, and he lived in Connecticut—they couldn't be further apart. But the knowing did not go away, so she booked a flight. Blossom had to reschedule her flight once and almost canceled, but she knew deep down inside that it was vital she go see him.

Her brother picked her up from the airport, and they drove down to their dad's house. When they got there, Blossom's dad was his normal self. She wasn't sure why she'd had to see him, but she knew the trip was important. She couldn't explain it to her brother, but he didn't even question it. They were all happy to be able to hang out for the short time they were together.

As soon as Blossom left her dad's house to go back to California, she cried. Hard. In the car and on the plane, all the way home. She didn't know exactly why she was crying at the time, but she knows now. It was the last time Blossom would ever see her dad. He unexpectedly passed away shortly after her visit. Thankfully, she listened to her claircognizance—her intuition had been the driving force to get her to Connecticut.

We are blessed by our intuition in so many ways. As Blossom shared, she was able to see her dad one last time. That is a memory she wouldn't trade for the world. We may not know what our claircognizant gifts are trying to relay to us, either at the time or even after. It's more important to recognize we are receiving an impression. Intuition will always be there. Epiphanies are like a bell ringing to get your attention, and your perception of these events or knowings can lead to expanding your intuition exponentially.

Intuition is not always black or white. Knowing what your intuition is trying to impart is not always natural—intuition can even be downright confusing. Yes, it's possible that you will have absolutely no idea why you're getting the impressions you're getting, but it's important to pay attention nonetheless. Ask the universe for some more information to help you decipher what is happening. All you can do is try! The more open you are to your intuition as you experience it, the more you'll be able to comprehend.

Esme

Esme worked as a director at a large nonprofit. She'd been there for about ten years and was done. She'd outgrown the job. It had been good while it lasted, but it was too much: she traveled too much, worked too many weekends, and gave up too many nights. She started searching for a new job—a job outside of the nonprofit world, a job that wouldn't have her working overtime.

In the midst of looking, Esme had a knowing. She knew she needed to stay where she was. She got mad. She didn't want to stay! She was ready to leave it all behind and spend more time with her kids, her husband, and her friends. She didn't feel fulfilled in her position anymore. She'd accomplished everything she could at her current job, and she wanted out. Though she desperately wanted the change, she knew, down to her core, that she needed to stay, at least for a while.

Soon after that claircognizant insight, Esme was offered a new position at the same company. This position was more to her liking, though it still wasn't exactly what she wanted. However, Esme knew that she needed to continue at the nonprofit, in her director position, but in a new capacity. Still, she had no idea why her intuition was telling her not to leave.

Then the bottom dropped out. Esme had been helping her husband stay sober, and unbeknownst to her, he'd relapsed. It got so bad that he had to go to rehab. During that time, she alone had to provide for her family. Though it wasn't easy, she made it work. Then the other shoe dropped—Esme was diagnosed with breast cancer. Her current employers were very sympathetic to her situation. Actually, they were a nonprofit that supported cancer research, so they were extremely helpful and gave Esme all the work flexibility they could. Now, Esme is cancer-free!

Claircognizance is one of those pesky intangibles that we have to learn to trust, even when we have nothing to substantiate it. I'm not going to lie—it's tough! But when you're experiencing claircognizance, you just *know* something, in spite of the fact you have no data to verify it. Once you have gone through a few situations where you've either listened to or ignored your intuition, you'll be more open to trusting it. Our confidence in our abilities increases the more we use them.

EXERCISE Family Ties

Having support from your family can contribute to the intuitive connections you have with them. We can learn from our intuition when our loved ones need us, or when we need them. If your bond isn't very strong, this can make it difficult to believe in the psychic bridge between yourself and your loved ones. One way to strengthen this connection, even if you don't feel you have as much support as you'd like, is to create a metaphysical link.

First, make sure your connection is intended to be positive; negativity doesn't serve you or your intuition. And this is important: if it's someone who may have an issue with what you're doing, ask their permission first. You never want to exert your will on someone else.

Then, imagine a string. Feel this string stretching from you to the loved one that you want to connect to more. Know that this string can be tightened up by gently turning a wheel that is located at the very top of your head (your crown chakra); if the string feels too taut, you can let some of it back out. Once you feel the connection and it's comfortable, you can end the exercise, knowing that the metaphysical connection is there any time you need support. All you have to do is tune in to your intuition.

JP

High school students JP and Stacy were at a party. There were a lot of people there; some they knew, and some they didn't. A guy they'd never seen before came up to them and gave them a joint. JP and Stacy had smoked pot before, so this was no big deal. They thought, *Why not? It's free.* After the girls smoked, they felt really good. For some reason, it felt different than the marijuana high they were used to. They laughed that he must have a really good hookup.

The next day, they saw the guy again, the same one that had given them the joint at the party. He asked how they liked the pot, and they agreed it was great stuff.

He said, "I can take you back to my place and give you some more if you want?"

He was nice and seemed totally cool. But for some reason, JP got a weird vibe from him. She knew, right then and there, that there was something wrong. She thought about it, and she intuitively knew that if she went, there would be no going back. Even though she wanted to feel that good again, she said no. She didn't understand it at the time. After all, it was just pot. But she knew, deep down in her soul, that it would change her life for the worse.

"Stacy, I don't think it's a good idea," she whispered.

"Oh, come on, JP. It's the guy. You know, everyone knows him. Nothing's going to happen," she replied.

Stacy took him up on his offer; JP didn't. JP ended up okay, but Stacy ended up addicted to crack. Though they hadn't known it at the time, there was crack in the joint JP and Stacy smoked at the party. When Stacy went with the guy, she ended up smoking more.

Last JP heard, Stacy was still struggling with substance abuse. If JP hadn't listened to her intuition, she could've ended up in the same situation. While JP hadn't been immediately sure what she was experiencing with her claircognizance, she knew it was profound, and she's very glad she listened to her soul's warning.

Barb

Students aren't the only ones who get intuitive nudges. Teachers pay attention to their metaphysical instincts as well. Barb experienced this while teaching at a private school. She'd been there for a few years and loved the students and the staff. She followed normal school protocol and felt, for the most part, that the teaching parameters were working well for the kids.

All that changed one day when Barb knew, intuitively, that the school needed a new program, a new way to teach a specific math lesson. She felt this different, intuitive way of teaching that she could develop would help the students learn through hands-on experience. Barb felt strongly that integrating experiential learning would allow the students to catch on to math concepts quickly. She also knew the program her students needed hadn't been created before, and therefore, it had never been tested. But something in her mind was telling her she needed to push forward; she even knew what the program needed to be. So, Barb developed the program with no hesitation. When she was finished, she presented it to the powers that be, and it was met with great applause.

Barb knew the program would help her students learn, and it did. That private school still has the program Barb designed in effect to this day. The students enrolled at Barb's school definitely got lucky. They now benefit from a unique learning experience that may end up being life-altering.

Tracy

Tracy's experience was also life-altering, though profound in a totally different way. She'd been working at a bank and was getting tired of seeing greed from businesses and people. She was becoming disenchanted with the fundamental, corporate side of life.

On one particularly stressful day, a friend asked Tracy for a ride to a massage therapy class. Tracy agreed, and when they arrived, Tracy's intuition told her to go into the presentation with her friend. Though she'd had no intention of attending, it felt like she was exactly where she should be—she just knew she was in the right place. Tracy signed up immediately. The following week, Tracy began taking classes to become a massage therapist. It felt good. Once again, she knew she was in the right place.

When Tracy began to work with clients, she intuitively knew exactly where and how to work on them. Her instructor asked her why she was focusing on certain spots.

She answered, "I just know where they need my healing the most."

When Tracy initially signed up for massage therapist classes, she had no intention of actually leaving her job. But as soon as she finished her training, she knew it was time to move forward with her life, and she started working full-time as a massage therapist. Since then, Tracy has added a variety of healing modalities to her bag of tricks, and she very much enjoys working with her clients.

EXERCISE Using Automatic Writing

When trying to make a decision, big or small, it can be beneficial to tune in to your claircognizant abilities. Using automatic writing, or intuitive writing, is one way to do this. Simply stated, this means letting your pen write down whatever comes to you without thinking about it or questioning it.

Grab a pen and paper before answering the following questions. In this case, the questions revolve around your career, but automatic writing can be used in all sorts of situations.

+ Do you want to work for someone else? Or yourself?
+ What do you feel connected to?
+ What makes you feel connected to yourself?
+ What do you want out of your life?
+ What skills do you have?
+ How can you best use your gifts?
+ How can you use your skill set in a more fulfilling way?

Emma

There are so many reasons to pay attention to your intuition. The psychic impressions are valuable: they may lead you to change careers, to save a life, or even to your special someone—even if it's not who you were expecting.

Emma, a college student, found out there was a renegade party coming up. These parties in the forest were not unusual—she knew of at least one a month. She'd been to a bunch of them and had fun, but they weren't vital to her life, or even to having a good time in college. However, this renegade party was different; she didn't know why, but Emma knew she had to be at this particular party.

None of her friends could go with her, so Emma decided to go alone, which was totally outside of her comfort zone. As soon as she walked into the gathering, she saw her ex-boyfriend, whom she hadn't seen in about a year. Emma's heart did a little flutter. They reconnected and rekindled their love. The two of them just celebrated eight months together. Emma's intuition had told her this renegade party was important, and now she knows why.

Gwen

Recognition often comes after the fact—sometimes the impressions you receive aren't easily identified until things have played out. That's not always the case when following your intuition, of course, but you should always pay attention to your soul's messages.

College students Gwen and her girlfriend, Sue, moved to Gwen's mom's house in Maine for the summer. They had a fantastic setup: they were able to live together without having to rent a place for the summer. During their stay, Sue decided to head down to Connecticut for a night to go visit a friend. Gwen was invited, but she had to work, so she stayed behind and told Sue to have a great time.

At 2:00 a.m., Gwen woke up with a terrible feeling in her stomach. She knew something was wrong. She tried to call Sue, but her phone was off. Gwen did her best to relax until she could get a hold of Sue, but she was unable to go back to sleep.

When Sue came back home the next day, Gwen asked what was going on.

Sue replied, "Nothing. What are you talking about?"

Gwen knew she was lying.

"You aren't being honest. Just own it. Tell me what happened," Gwen challenged.

Sue finally gave in and told Gwen she was breaking up with her. Gwen demanded to know what had happened. At first Sue told her it was just not working out and that she had gone away to talk to her friend about it. When Gwen pressed her some more, she admitted she had cheated on her.

Naturally, Gwen wanted to know more. She asked, "What time were you actually cheating on me? Like, what time were you in bed with someone else?"

Gwen told Sue she was going to write down a time on a piece of paper and then wanted to know the approximate time.

"Fine. It was around 2:00 a.m.," Sue grudgingly told her.

When Gwen flipped the paper over, it was revealed that she had written 2:00 a.m. She knew it! When she woke at 2:00 a.m., she had known something was wrong, but she hadn't known exactly what it was until Sue came home and broke up with her.

Relationships can be tricky. That's why it's so important to pay attention to your senses. Your perceptions may not be easily spelled out for you, especially if they are trying to alert you to something you don't want to deal with or even know.

Rachel

Rachel was unaware of the strong psychic connection she had with her husband, Karl, until one not-so-great night. She described it to me as a turning point in her own intuitive awareness. Rachel had gone out to dinner and drinks with Karl and another couple. They had steak and a couple of drinks over the course of a few hours. Eventually, Rachel and her friend Sara told the guys they should get going, but the husbands decided they would stay for a few more drinks and then Uber home.

Rachel left with a bad feeling, though she wasn't sure what it meant. Sara dropped her off at home, and Rachel put the kids to sleep and went to bed herself. At 1:15 a.m., she woke up with a pit in her stomach. Out of nowhere, she knew she had to get up and get dressed and wake her oldest. She told her oldest daughter that there was an emergency and she and Daddy had to run to the hospital, but all would be okay and they would be back soon.

Sure enough, five minutes later, as Rachel was getting ready to go, Karl stumbled in. She quietly told him in a no-nonsense voice, "We're going to the hospital."

When he asked why, she told him to look in the mirror. His face was bleeding near his ear. It was clear that something had happened.

When they got to the hospital, the doctor in the emergency room told them they were lucky it was a slow night. He shared that although it was a bit after 2:00 a.m., it was usually a very busy time because that's when the bars closed. The doctor took a look at Karl and determined that he needed nine stitches.

By now, Karl had sobered up and come clean on what happened. Turns out he had gotten mad at someone at the bar who was razzing him, and Karl threatened to knock the guy out. Instead of leading Karl out, the bouncers tackled him. He ended up on the ground, on top of his own broken glass.

Trusting claircognizant vibes can be difficult. They're usually even more difficult to trust when they are sending messages about someone else, not you. Generally, in those instances when your claircognizant awareness is coming through about someone else, it is often because it also affects you.

· · · · · · — · · · · · ·
PONDER THIS
CLAIRCOGNIZANCE
FOR YOU OR SOMEONE ELSE?

Take a moment to think about any intuitive impressions you've had in the past—they may have been current or something you experienced years ago. Then, take a moment to ponder how these knowings impacted your life. You might instantly know the answer, or it may still be a bit cloudy.

When claircognizance is about someone else, it can be hard to do anything but prepare yourself for what may be coming. If you feel comfortable, you can share what you perceived with the other person. They may recognize what you are telling them.

Ultimately, respecting the message your claircognizance is imparting to you is the best way to understand the initial vibe.

Jenelle

Jenelle was headed to an appointment with her therapist, Eleanor. She loved this woman. At this point, Eleanor was like family— Jenelle had been seeing her for twenty years! Eleanor had been there through all of the ups and downs of her life, including when Jenelle made the incredible decision to adopt her beautiful daughter. She'd also helped Jenelle through the death of her mom, whom she'd been extremely close to. Eleanor was her therapist, yes, but she was also her person, her confidante, and her friend. That's why when Jenelle walked into Eleanor's office, she was upset—her intuition had told her a sad truth.

Eleanor took one look at her and asked, "Uh-oh. What's wrong, Jenelle?"

"Well …" Jenelle started.

She sat down and got teary-eyed.

"What's going on, Jenelle? Is your daughter okay?" Eleanor asked.

"It's not that. It's …" She couldn't say it without getting super emotional.

"Just breathe. Take a minute," Eleanor consoled, thinking something had happened.

"You're leaving me!" Jenelle shouted, rather loudly.

"What? What are you talking about?" Eleanor asked.

"I know it. I don't know how I know, but I know it!" she continued.

"I'm not leaving you," her therapist replied thoughtfully. "But how did you know I was retiring?"

Jenelle was gobsmacked. Not only was she right, but she knew before Eleanor had told her patients or anyone else in her practice. Turns out, she'd just decided to retire the week before, and she was waiting to tell her patients until the end of the month; she had planned to give them two months' notice as well as referrals to trusted colleagues.

Ultimately, Eleanor was right: she wasn't leaving Jenelle. Their relationship has now changed from therapist and patient to dear friends. They are on an even plane and are able to hang out and do things they were unable to do before. Though Jenelle's claircognizant gifts had alerted her to the change, she happily discovered there was a better outcome than she expected.

Ethan

Ethan, a police officer, was known for finding stolen cars. It was what he did: he worked in the auto theft division. Now, there's a difference between a couple of kids who steal a car to go for a joyride and the professionals. The professionals have an agenda and usually change something about the look of the car to avoid detection if they aren't shipped to a new area immediately after the theft.

The "professional stolens," as Ethan called them, will have all the vehicle identification numbers changed; there's no way to know the car has been stolen unless you run the VIN. So, as a hindrance to the cops and even to avoid proof, the professionals have a network where they can add or use an old VIN on a car so they can get them registered. This is an important step because then the license plates will actually be registered to the car in the motor vehicle system.

One day, Ethan and a young officer were making their way back to the station. She told him she'd never made a stolen car arrest. He thought that over for about half a second and then told her they'd get one that night. He just knew it was going to happen; his claircognizance assured him that it was inevitable.

A minute later, they stopped at a red light.

"The vehicle in front of us is a stolen," he told her calmly.

"What? How do you know? Was it on the list?" she asked him.

"I just know. Let's find out how good my intuition is," Ethan answered with a chuckle.

On went the lights and the siren. The car in front of them pulled over and while his fellow officer asked for license and registration, he checked out the VIN. He found the numbers had all been changed. Turns out it had been stolen the previous year, from another state. The driver was oblivious that she had purchased a stolen car.

When the officer asked how he knew, Ethan told her, "I don't know how. I just did."

· · · · · · — · · · · · ·

PONDER THIS
CLAIRCOGNIZANT OR NOT?

An easy way to determine if you are having a flash of claircognizance when answering a question is to ask yourself the following:

+ Did you know the answer without evidentiary proof?
+ Did you answer with absolute certainty?
+ Were you surprised that you knew the answer because you don't know how or why you knew?

If you answered yes to these questions, signs point to you using your claircognizant gifts. While of course it's not always a guarantee, these questions are a good starting point.

Tanya

Tanya, a theater and music director, was driving home from rehearsal with her son, Trip. They were discussing her latest play.

"I feel like it's going really well. Everyone seems to be grasping their roles, and with a few tweaks, I think it could be a great show!" Tanya said.

"I agree. It seems like everyone knows what they're doing. Maybe a little more background sound during the down times?" he replied.

As they continued discussing the play, Tanya suddenly swerved to get off the interstate.

"Whoa, Mom! What are you doing? I thought we were going home?!" Trip exclaimed as he held on.

"We are—I don't have any idea why I'm getting off the exit."

Usually, Tanya took Interstate 91 all the way home. For some reason, she knew, in an instant, that she needed to get off and drive a different way home. For Tanya, this was very unusual, if only for the fact that she hated driving through New Haven at this time of the night. It took way too long, and there was entirely too much traffic. However, she knew she had to do it.

"Okay, Mom," Trip said, looking at her funny.

As they were getting off at the exit, they saw four cop cars flying by on I-91. They watched incredulously, then looked at each other. Later that evening, they saw on the news there'd been a nasty accident right past the exit where Tanya pulled off. That was all she needed to know in order to recognize her intuitive GPS system had indeed worked in their favor.

Sometimes You Just Know

Knowing can be a tricky thing. Sometimes it feels like you're just making something up. We often look for a reason to discount our claircognizance because it can be hard to trust it without additional evidence. True claircognizance shows up suddenly, and though you usually have nothing to back it up, it is 100 percent real. You just know, in spite of the fact you have no data to verify your knowing.

A good way to determine if a knowing is really your intuition is to ponder how it appeared. Was it immediate? Was it strong? Did it make you wonder how you suddenly knew something? That's usually a telltale sign that a message is indeed your soul giving you explicit information.

As you've read, there's nothing your intuition can't do for you. When you start believing in your claircognizance, even with the absence of any tangible evidence, you'll notice it starts to happen more often. Trusting your knowing can bring you a sense of calm.

PRO TIP

Claircognizance can be confusing because you may know something suddenly, with nothing to back it up. This is totally normal!

Chapter 4
CLAIRVOYANCE

Clairvoyance does not mean psychic! I can't tell you how many times I've heard the word *clairvoyant* used in place of the word *psychic*. A psychic can be clairvoyant, but not every psychic has this ability. Clairvoyance is merely one of the psychic or intuitive senses, and it means "clear sight."

Using Clear Sight

This is the ability to see intuitive visions in your mind. More often than not, these visions will be through your third eye, which is located in the middle of your forehead, slightly above and in the middle of your eyebrows.

Lisa Anne Rooney

Lisa Anne Rooney uses her intuitive and mediumship gifts when working with clients through her coaching business. She imparts a variety of methods in her book, *A Survival Guide for Those Who*

Have Psychic Abilities and Don't Know What to Do with Them. She shared with me that it took her a while to realize she had been using clairvoyance from a young age:

> Although I've had many clairvoyant messages over the years, the one that stands out the most is about my first book. Since I was young child, I would have visions of myself writing; those visions grew over the years and became much more detailed. I saw myself in different locations, writing and writing. I would be laughing, crying—and at the core of the emotion was fulfillment. As the visions evolved, I started to see a book. I would be holding it, flipping through it. I started to see the color of the cover and the images on the front. Dragonflies would be flying all around me.
>
> The funny part is I would have these visions, but I never took them as a message. I took them as a pipe dream. Even when I decided to sit down and write my first manuscript and go through the publishing process, I didn't connect the two. (Like many people, when it comes to getting messages for ourselves, we tend to ignore them.) It wasn't until I received a copy of my book from Llewellyn that it hit me. Holding my book in my hands, I realized it was the exact color I saw in my visions, and on the front cover was a dragonfly! I knew then that those visions were a message about what was going to happen.
>
> —Lisa Anne Rooney

Even professionals sometimes struggle with whether a vision is intuitive or not. How a vision appears to you can help you discern whether it's your intuition or imagination. Usually, intuitive visions are internal. If a vision is connected to your emotions or is based on your own personal beliefs, that can indicate it's one of those non-psychic visions. In other words, it's just something connected to you, personally—it's quite possible you are seeing an outcome that you want versus a legit intuitive vision. That sort of vision could be your imagination, or even wishful thinking.

EXERCISE Using Your Imagination to Utilize Your Clairvoyance

Are you able to clearly see something from physical reality in your mind's eye? Practice using your memory to conjure up pictures in your mind. Right now, think of what your home looks like. See what the outside looks like. Envision the doors, the siding, the windows. Look at the colors. Being able to imagine your home without physically looking at it can help you hone your internal vision. Plus, this supports your ability to differentiate between your imagination and intuitive visions, as you will be familiar with how your imagination presents.

Jack

Jack had a vision when his wife, Mandy, was pregnant. Up until that point, Mandy's pregnancy had been going fine—she'd had some ups and downs, but nothing concerning. One day when Jack was at work, he received a call no one wants to get when they are expecting a baby: Mandy was on her way to the hospital. Something had happened.

Apparently, Mandy had felt something, started bleeding, and went into distress. She called 911 immediately, which brought officers and an ambulance to the house. Jack knew the ambulance attendants; they were friends. So, he called them as he ran out the door, but they refused to tell him what happened. From the minute he jumped in his car, he knew that his family was going to be okay. He kept getting visions of Mandy and the baby, happy in the hospital bed, and then happy at home. He had no worries about it.

When Jack arrived at the hospital, the doctor, a close friend of his sister's, walked by him without even acknowledging him. After asking around, a staff member informed Jack that Mandy had placenta previa, and they had immediately taken her into the operating room. Thankfully, the surgery went well and they were able to save both Mandy and the newborn baby.

A couple days later, Jack saw the doctor, and he asked why he'd been ignored at the hospital. After all, the doctor had been to their house before! He'd figured the doctor was busy, rushing to save Mandy, but to turn the other way as he went by seemed a bit much. Jack was hurt and confused.

The doctor responded, "I'm sorry, Jack. I didn't want to face you yet. Neither your wife nor your baby should have lived. I just couldn't deal with that at the moment. I had to get to work and didn't want to talk to you because I just didn't have anything good to say right then."

"That's okay. I knew everyone was going to be fine. On the way to the hospital, I saw in my mind's eye an image of Mandy holding a perfect baby, and I just knew my vision was real and that they were both going to not only make it, but they were going to be great— I wasn't worried at all!" Jack answered.

The doctor was shocked, but it made sense. When he'd seen Jack, he'd had a smile on his face. Most husbands would have been totally freaked out! The doctor had thought that was strange at the time, but now he knew why.

Jack's clairvoyance allowed him to see that his family would not only survive, but thrive. This was the first vision he ever had. He's continued receiving different images through what he now recognizes as his third eye; he trusts his clairvoyance. It keeps him calm in even the most stressful situations.

Linda

Frequently, when we are faced with life-altering situations—ours or someone else's—our intuition kicks in to aid with our processing. It can help us make decisions, prepare for distress or emotional pain, or even let us know everything will be okay. Once you trust that your intuition will feel different than your imagination, you won't be left scratching your head as often.

Another thing to pay attention to is that intuitive visions are often symbolic, as in Linda's case. Linda was head nurse of the critical care unit. She had been there for almost twenty years and had been a nurse for about thirty. She was more than capable of taking care of the patients in her charge and was always there to lend a hand to the other nurses and their patients when needed. She also worked well with the doctors; they trusted her to tend to their patients beyond what was actually required of her position. Linda was a brilliant medical professional, and she would have went on to become a doctor had her finances and circumstances allowed for it.

On this particular day, Linda was taking care of one of her patients when she saw an order for a specific medicine from the doctor. She immediately saw an image of a coffin. That image told her these meds were going to kill the patient. Linda checked in again with her intuition and asked for validation, as she needed to be sure. Again, she saw an image of a coffin, this time a different one.

Linda was no stranger to intuitive guidance and listened to her intuition often. She was aware that she needed to pay attention to her clairvoyance, so instead of giving her patient the medicine the doctor ordered, she called him. She wouldn't acquiesce until she got the doctor to come back up to the unit. He did, and immediately the doctor realized his mistake—the patient was allergic to the medicine. The doctor thanked Linda profusely. Without Linda's intervention, the patient would indeed have died. Linda was grateful that her psychic visions had guided her in the right direction, and this situation served as a reminder to always take note when she had clairvoyant impressions.

Sometimes what we see in our mind will not be a literal representation of what our intuition is trying to share with us. Often, it is symbolic. For instance, when clients ask me if I feel their mother coming through in a session, I regularly depend on symbolism for my answer. If I see an image of a baseball field, I know their mother is there—not because she played baseball, but because it is a symbol for me that means "Mom," as my own mother began watching baseball games all the time toward the end of her life. I immediately see this symbol if the client's mother is with us.

EXERCISE What Do You See?

What image comes to mind right now when you think of your mother? Did you see something in your mind's eye? How about your father? Try this for your brother, sister, husband, wife, child, etc. You may see their image in your mind, but then take it a step further and think about what other images may represent them. See those symbols clearly. Remember them.

We don't always see a clear, sustained image when it comes to third eye visions. We might see an image flash like a postcard or a Polaroid picture. They can be symbolic, or they may be more literal.

When I asked my daughter to imagine an image of me in her mind's eye, she first saw a picture of how I really look. Then, I told her to imagine an image that represents me. I told her the image in her mind might stay the same, or it might change. This time, she saw an image of a sun, as if it was drawn by a child. I love that! Now my daughter knows she may get flashes of "me" in different ways.

Lori

Lori, a director of planning and development, was used to seeing real, tangible images in her work. What she wasn't used to as much were intuitive visions. Lori totally believed that other people were able to see things psychically, but she hadn't experienced clairvoyance herself. Then, one day while she was at her mother's house, she had a couple of visions that made her nervous.

Lori had felt unsettled all day, but she wasn't sure why until she saw an image in her mind's eye. A picture of snow flying in all directions appeared in her head. At first, she thought it was just because she was thinking of her husband; he'd gotten brand new skis for Christmas and, living in Vermont, they were both used to taking a few hours here and there to hit the slopes. At the moment, he was off trying out his new equipment.

Lori then had a flash of another image show up in her mind. This time, she saw her husband lying on the snow. To ease her nerves, Lori tried to reach her husband on his cell phone, but he wasn't answering. She texted then, asking him if he was all right. Again, no response.

Another image showed up, this time a red cross, which is often symbolic of first aid. Now, Lori knew something was happening or was about to happen. At this point, she was positive that her husband was going to have a skiing accident.

She tried getting in touch again, this time leaving a message. "Hey, hon. It's me. I don't want to scare you or anything, but maybe you should pack it up and call it a day. I'm feeling like you're going to get hurt or something. Please call me back!"

After she left the message, Lori let it go for a bit and concentrated on hanging out with her mom. After about an hour went by, she got a phone call from her husband.

"Where are you? Are you okay?" she said immediately.

"Well, funny story," he started.

"Oh no, don't tell me…"

"So, I was in an ambulance when you called. I wiped out, pretty badly, and they had to call an ambulance. I'm in the hospital right now, but I'm okay, don't worry."

"Umm, what do you mean you're in the hospital right now? And you were in an ambulance?" Lori replied, her voice having risen a bit.

"I dislocated my shoulder. Nothing's broken and I'm fine. I am going to need a ride, though," he told her.

Because she'd seen visions of his accident, Lori was prepared for this call. Even though she hadn't physically been there, she saw enough (both symbolically and literally) to let her know something was happening. Afterward, she told me, she almost felt a sense of relief—not because he'd gotten hurt, but because it wasn't as terrible as it could have been.

When I was collecting stories for this book, I expected most stories would be like Lori's. I believed they would have happy endings, or at least have a positive twist at the end. And most of them did. But every once in a while, I collected a story that leaned a bit negative. It can be fantastic when your intuition is right—it makes you feel great! With that being said, those times when you know something negative is going to occur, and then it does: they're not so much fun. Whether your clairvoyance is showing you something positive or negative, it's equally as important to pay attention.

Precognitive Visions

Precognitive visions may or may not show you something you recognize or understand. Whether or not they make sense in the moment, they are still real. Be open to what you're seeing and allow it to ruminate in your third eye.

One way to decipher what you're seeing is to try and look beyond the main imagery. If the vision has already passed and you're not seeing anything more, try and remember what colors, shapes, and other clues your vision showed you. Also, if you saw a person that you know in your vision, note how old they looked. Did they look about the same as they do now? This can help you figure out how far in the future you are seeing things play out.

EXERCISE Precognitive Vision

Perhaps you've had a precognitive flash before. If so, fantastic! Even if you have not had a precognitive vision, this exercise can help you see what's to come.

Think about something coming up for you that you are curious about. This could be a date or a meeting at work, or maybe it's something to do with your family or an upcoming event. Whatever it is, just think about an event and name it. For example, "blind date," or "work happy hour," or "my friend's wedding," etc. This doesn't have to be a fancy name— choose something your intuition can grab ahold of.

Go somewhere you can relax and close your eyes. Then take a deep breath. Breathe in clearing, positive energy. Exhale any debris or negativity you may be holding on to. Continue doing this until you're totally relaxed.

Next, focus on the name you assigned to whatever event you wish to see. Pay attention to any visions that may show up as you think. If you don't see anything right away, that's fine. Continue to focus on the name you've chosen for this exercise. Whatever you see, don't discount it; even the strangest visions may be clairvoyance.

After you've finished seeing any images, write them down. You can determine what they might mean to you as a whole when you're all done. Also write down what you think the outcome of this event will be based on your vision. Set this paper aside so you can refer back to it in the future.

Then, after the event has passed, compare what actually happened with what you saw through your precognitive sight. Were your visions accurate? Was your possible outcome accurate? You may find your vision was accurate but your possible outcome wasn't, or vice versa—that's okay. As you develop further, you may discover you're better at one or the other. Write a few sentences about how accurate you were.

Repeat this process each time you work with your clairvoyance. Are there any patterns you're noticing? If your visions are usually accurate but the outcomes you drew from them are not, perhaps you should rethink how you determine what your visions mean. This could also be an indication that you shouldn't try to put things together, instead trusting the visions to play out.

Jolene

Jolene had five sisters. One of them, Melody, was struggling with her sobriety. After having been to rehab multiple times to no avail, Jolene and her sisters decided to financially support Melody going to rehab again. Jolene's sisters decided they wanted to clean and organize Melody's house before she got out of rehab as a special surprise.

However, Jolene was convinced this would backfire on them. Her intuition showed her that this would *not* be appreciated: when Melody came home from rehab, she would yell at her sisters, mad that they had invaded her space. Jolene could see Melody clear as day, like a movie in high definition and full color, angry that her sisters had the audacity to "raid" her space.

Jolene's sisters ignored her intuitive warnings. Everyone agreed Melody would appreciate coming home to a clean house—everyone except Jolene. She just couldn't let go of her intuitive vision that everything would go wrong if they beautified the house.

When her sisters headed over to clean Melody's house, Jolene decided she wasn't going. She wanted nothing to do with it, believing that the images of Melody screaming at her were a prediction of what was to come. Her sisters thought Jolene was being lazy; they questioned whether she just didn't want to help them. All of the women were naturally very neat, including Jolene, so her sisters couldn't understand why she wouldn't want to help bring Melody's home up to their standards. She tried explaining her visions again, but they thought she was nuts. Jolene's sisters cleaned and organized Melody's home anyway.

The day Melody left rehab, Jolene and her sisters brought her home. Jolene's sisters were so excited to show Melody her house; they told her this was a new start for her, and they were there to help her in any way they could. But after Melody walked in and saw what they had done, she immediately looked to Jolene and asked why she thought she had the right to invade her space and clean the house. Even after Jolene told Melody she had nothing to do with it, she continued to give her a hard time. Melody didn't let up; she started to yell at Jolene.

Jolene looked to the rest of her sisters, who all looked a bit uneasy, and raised her hands and said, "I told you so!" Then, she left.

Unfortunately, Jolene's visions had come to fruition. The funny thing was, even though her sisters had been the ones to clean Melody's house, all the negativity had been directed toward Jolene, who hadn't even participated! Not every outcome can be avoided, even if we know it's coming. At least Jolene's premonition had prepared her.

Grayson

As I said earlier, not all stories have a happy ending. That's exactly what Grayson was afraid of. As he headed off to college, he worried about who he would meet and whether he would make any friends. And when he thought about the possibility of meeting a significant other, he saw a flash of a hockey player.

School started, and Grayson did make friends. Still, every time he thought about his future significant other, he saw an image of a hockey player. When he told his friends what he'd seen in his mind's eye, they asked if he was gay or bisexual, since their college only had a men's hockey team. Grayson told them he very much liked girls. He figured the vision probably meant he would become friends with some guys on the hockey team.

Until he met a girl from another college. What she told him next blew him away: her college had a women's ice hockey team, and she played on it! Grayson's vision came true. It's been over two years, and he's still dating his hockey player girlfriend!

Grayson's visions had a happy ending. Even though he did not understand his visions initially, he knew they were showing him something important. Hopefully Grayson's story encourages you to trust your own visions a little bit more.

Loretta

In talking with people from all walks of life and in all stages of life, I've heard so many stories of love and romance. It seems there is a connection between what the heart wants and what our intuition tries to get us to tap into.

Loretta, a licensed nurse, was newly divorced and a single mom. After work, she often took her kids to the local county club, which had a pool. While they swam, she walked the golf course, as there were not many golfers in the evenings. She often talked to God and the universe on her walks; she felt closest to her intuition during this time. One day, as Loretta walked to the top of a hill, she saw a vision of David—a guy she had gone to high school with but did not know well. He was in a black tuxedo, standing at what looked like an altar. Then the vision went away.

At the time of her vision, Loretta was dating someone else. She thought it was interesting that she'd had a vision of David, but she didn't think too much about it and quickly let it go—until they ran into each other at a store about a year later, both single, and began talking. Loretta and David discovered they were very interested in each other and were married two years after her vision.

It would be nice if everyone had a crystal ball to find their perfect partner. Well, with the help of our intuition, we kind of do! While we may not intuitively see exactly what we want to see, the more we embrace what our gifts are presenting to us, the more images we will receive. Stay open to all kinds of clairvoyant messages. When we block visions or push them away because they're not what we were hoping to see, we are shutting down our gifts.

Accepting what you see, even if you don't like it, can be beneficial—after all, it may have been shown to you for a reason you've not yet discovered. For example, you may be shown a subway not because your future love drives the train, but because they are an electrical engineer. Stay curious and open-minded!

EXERCISE Symbolic Imagery

It's time to create your own symbolic image reference guide. For now, we will be using clairvoyant imagery. Get a fresh notepad or open a blank document on your computer. At the top, write *Symbols*.

Next, write down the word *stop*. Then, pause and envision the first thing that comes to mind. Write down exactly what you saw. Repeat this process for each of the following words:

Go	Vacation
New	Career
Plenty of money	Financial problems
Love	Healthy relationship
Unhealthy relationship	Exercise
Writing/journaling	Home/house
Friendship	Danger
Happiness/joy	Gift
Career change	Move
Deceased loved ones	Alert
Contentedness	Emotional
Kind/caring	Accident
Strength	Powerful

You may see your associated images the next time your third eye is trying to communicate with you. When you see the images you recorded, you can trust your intuition and immediately figure out what it's trying to tell you.

Markus

Markus was a soldier stationed at Camp Lejeune. He decided he wanted a motorcycle, even though his mother had told him he should never get one. Once, she'd had a vision of him in a really bad motorcycle accident and had never gotten it out of her head. Of course, Markus didn't listen to her and bought one anyway.

When she found out, his mom said, "Get rid of it! You'll kill yourself!"

Markus responded, "Mom, I'm in the Marines. I'm pretty sure the bike is not what will kill me."

It wasn't that Markus didn't believe in intuition; he just figured all moms felt that way about motorcycles. So, he kept the bike. His mom did the only thing she knew to do: she jumped into a pickup and drove down to get it. After the motorcycle was loaded into the back of the truck, she brought it home and sold it. She gave the money to Markus and made him promise not to buy another bike. At that point, she thought her vision had been avoided and everything was going to be fine.

After Markus got out of the service, he moved in with his girlfriend. When he told her he used to have a bike, she convinced him to buy a new one. She loved motorcycles, and Markus still did too. Again, his mom begged him to get rid of it. Again, he didn't listen. He should have. Unfortunately, his mother was right. Shortly after he got his new bike, he was in a terrible accident. His mother had intuitively seen the exact accident long before it happened.

The motorcycle accident nearly killed Markus; he had to be helicoptered to the hospital. Before the phone rang, his mom knew. She was actually shocked that he was alive and rushed to the hospital to see what was happening. When she arrived, the ambulance crew, the helicopter crew, an officer, and personnel from two hospitals all told her it was a miracle Markus survived the accident; they all agreed he shouldn't have made it.

Alas, Markus didn't make it out unscathed. He endured over thirty surgeries after the accident and, sadly, lost one of his legs. Thankfully, he didn't lose his life. Since the accident, Markus has adapted to his new reality extremely well. For that, everyone is tremendously grateful.

Hanna

Hanna was a single mom of three boys. She had been dating Derrick for some time, and they were both sure they were headed for marriage; they were in love, and Derrick was a great addition to Hanna's family. Everything was going great—and then Hanna had a vision.

In Hanna's vision, she saw Derrick. But the image she saw of him was just his head, his hands, and his feet—no body. It was strange, but she was a big believer in paying attention to her intuition. She immediately feared Derrick would become paralyzed somehow. She couldn't get the vision out of her mind; for a while, she contemplated telling Derrick that even if he became paralyzed, she'd always love him.

Eight years went by. Derrick and Hanna were married and the boys were all grown up; they were finishing high school and heading off to college. All was going well. Then, Derrick started feeling tired all the time. He had no energy or desire to do anything. Hanna and Derrick started having little arguments—she wanted to get out and do things together, but felt like he never did. She wondered if it was something she did.

Then, Hanna remembered the vision she had had all those years ago. She told Derrick he needed to go to the doctor and get checked out. Sure enough, there was something wrong. Derrick was diagnosed with a rare disease: adult-onset muscular dystrophy. The doctor told them that this disease presented like a slow-progressing

ALS. But for Hanna and Derrick, it wasn't slow enough. Within a couple of years, Derrick's disease caused him to lose control of his muscles. He was just about paralyzed and living only with the help of breathing machines. Hanna took care of him until he passed. She knew, looking back, her vision was truly an indicator of what was going to happen. She'd caught a clairvoyant glimpse of the future.

Bea

Your precognitive visions may not be about you. Intuitive visions are often about people we know, loved ones, or events that are coming up. But remember, other people won't always believe your intuitive premonitions—it's more common than not for others to doubt us.

Bea dealt with this firsthand. Her son was going on a youth trip for a week to help build homes in rural Kentucky. Bea had a vision that the hotel that had been booked was not a good one for kids; in her mind's eye, she saw that they were going to be staying at a hotel that was mostly used by truckers. In her vision, she also saw sex workers and knew they would be around the hotel as well. This was not a suitable environment for a bus full of middle school and high school students.

Bea contacted the church and told them what she believed they could expect at the hotel. They told her it was too late to change hotels and that everything would be fine. She offered to do the work, to cancel the reservation and find them somewhere else to stay, but they essentially told her she was being silly and should let it go. Bea was *not* happy; she'd had intuitive visions in the past, so she knew to trust what she saw.

In addition to what she'd already seen, Bea had another vision: on Thursday all hell would break loose with the kids, and things would be really bad. Once again, she contacted the church to share her worries, and once again, the church discounted her concerns and refused to change hotels.

"I'm telling you, it's not what you're expecting. It's going to be nothing but problems if we send our kids there. The other parents are definitely not going to approve and are going to be very upset when they find out," Bea insisted.

"I understand your concerns, Bea, but it really will be fine. Besides, they leave tomorrow. There's no time to change the reservations, nor do we feel there is a need. I'm sorry that you believe in your '*visions*,' but you know only God can show us the way," the woman replied.

Finally, Bea told her son about her visions, but he insisted he wanted to go on the trip despite her fears. Ultimately, she let him go, knowing there would be many adults from the church on the trip as well. Still, as she packed him up and sent him off, Bea reminded him not to do drugs or accept sex from strangers.

Sure enough, her son and several other children were propositioned in the parking lot shortly after they arrived at the hotel. In addition to sex workers, there were also drug dealers wandering around the hotel, and they tried really hard to sell to the kids when the adults weren't around.

On Thursday night, two days after they arrived, a bunch of the kids were taken to the hospital. They had bought and done drugs—mostly just marijuana, but some had done cocaine. Bea's son was the one who had taken responsibility and contacted the volunteers in charge, who then called an ambulance. Almost every kid on the trip got into a huge amount of trouble, including Bea's son. Even though he swore he didn't do any drugs on the trip, Bea's son had said the drugs were his. He explained to his mother that he had done so to protect another student.

"I knew, intuitively, that this particular kid was on scholarship. He would have been kicked out of his school if they found him doing drugs. He lives in a really bad area and the schools he would have to transfer to would be horrible for him," he explained to his mom.

After hearing this, Bea tuned in to her intuition again. With her third eye, she saw her son sitting out while others got high. He was hanging out with them, but not doing the drugs.

"You're a good kid," she told him.

Bea really had seen what was going to happen, and she was happy she had warned her son. She had even tried to warn the church volunteers, though she never received an apology. Bea had experienced a true premonition—there was no denying it. And, she had to admit, it felt good to be right. The adults she warned had to live with the fact that they hadn't listened. Luckily, no one was hurt.

· · · · · · — · · · · · ·
PONDER THIS
TRUSTING YOUR VISIONS

There will be times when a vision is hard to trust. And, more often than not, there will be times when others don't trust the vision you've shared with them. Think back to a time when this may have occurred. What was the outcome?

When someone doubts your vision, ask for another. Ask to see an image you are familiar with to validate or even invalidate what you believe your intuition is trying to tell you. If you are able to confirm your intuitive vision, great! It's not always necessary for others to trust in it.

When belief in your intuition is challenged, either by you or someone else, you can look at it as a time to strengthen your gifts. Continue practicing and developing your gifts—you may find your visions getting more detailed as you do!

Seeing Is Believing

Clairvoyance can be a scary word for those not in the know. But you know, don't you? You understand. Even if you didn't before, you do now.

Clairvoyance is not scary—it's actually a pretty cool intuitive gift! Although you may not recognize what you're seeing in your mind's eye, or you may be confused as to why you are seeing an image, this ability is like the universe giving you a present. As with any present, it should be appreciated. Nurture your gift so it can continue to grow and show you even more.

Practice will improve your proficiency at understanding your visions and might even increase the frequency of images you see. There are never any guarantees when it comes to intuitive gifts, but the one thing you can be sure of is this: clairvoyance is totally natural.

— ◉ —
PRO TIP

The images you see in your mind's eye may be more than your imagination. Pay attention to how your body responds to an image to determine if it's clairvoyance.

Chapter 5
CLAIRAUDIENCE

Clairaudience is clear intuitive hearing. The question I get asked all the time is "Does it have to be, like, full sentences?" There is often an expectation that clairaudience is a full-on conversation. However, that is extremely rare. For the most part, you won't hear complete sentences, let alone have a discussion.

Instead, you might experience clairaudience in different ways. Some people hear sounds, like car horns or bells ringing; for others, it's songs or song lyrics. Clairaudience may sound like a voice whispering a word. You have a much better chance of clairaudience showing up in this way than the conversation you may be hoping for. Whether you receive clairaudient messages in one way or multiple ways, you can feel fortunate.

Everyday Clairaudience

Clairaudience may happen before an important event or during an everyday moment. I've experienced clairaudience playing backgammon with my husband, Tom! We play every morning. At some point, we started keeping track of our wins and losses and were almost tied. (In fact, we've stayed within a ten-game spread since we started writing down our triumphs.) One morning, both of us had gotten into our home section, meaning the only thing we had left to do was to roll and take each individual piece off the board. I thought, *Aha! I am going to win!* I was beating him, having five pieces already off the board. But then, to my dismay, I heard the song "It's a Man's Man's Man's World" playing in my mind, and I knew he was going to win. Sure enough, he did!

After Tom won, I told him about hearing the song, and he giggled what I refer to as his evil little laugh and told me, "James Brown knows what's up!"

Victory was short lived—for him! The next morning, when we were just beginning to play backgammon, I heard "Man! I Feel Like a Woman!" by Shania Twain. I told him, right then and there, that he was going down, and of course, my clairaudient message was on point. As soon as I told him what I'd heard, he knew it was over for him.

Even though my clairaudience wasn't a complete conversation, the intuitive message was easily conveyed through song. And, more importantly, I understood it because it was so specific. I want to emphasize that not everyone hears songs, though. Occasionally, people do hear words or even sentences along with other noises. It all depends on how your clairaudience talks to you.

EXERCISE Listen to the Music

To strengthen your clairaudient muscles, try this exercise that will help you recognize your intuitive hearing.

Turn on some music. Try to play music you aren't as familiar with. Then, allow the lyrics to stand out to you. What are the lyrics saying? What are the exact words? Do they tell a story? Are they talking about a relationship? A situation? Consider this for a moment.

When the song ends, turn off the music. Ask the universe a question and allow a song to answer it for you. For example, if you ask whether or not you should move across the country and then hear John Denver's "Leaving on a Jet Plane" in your mind, this is your intuition trying to tell you it's a good idea, or there's a good chance you will. Alternatively, if you hear the song "Our House" by Crosby, Stills, Nash & Young, which exclaims that our house is a very fine house, then staying where you are may be more beneficial.

Think of another question you want answered and state it aloud. Then wait for a song to play in your mind. Does it make sense? Does it feel right? Did you hear singing? Remember, it's possible you won't hear lyrics. You may just hear sounds or random words; that's okay too. If you don't normally listen to music, clairaudient messages may not come to you in this way. Whatever sounds you hear are what you're meant to hear!

Cyndi Dale

Cyndi Dale, an energy worker, teacher, intuitive, and award-winning author of *Root Chakra* and more than thirty other books, shared that she has a voice that speaks to her, specifically in her right ear. One day, what she heard would inevitably change the trajectory of her life:

Quit your job. Start your company, I heard.

I was terrified. Sure, I believed in my intuition, but to simply stop working? I knew the Voice was instructing me to begin my psychic healing business, but I didn't feel ready. So, I bargained. I made a set of business cards for psychic healing and another for public relations consulting.

When I picked up the psychic healing cards, a card was taped to the end of the box. It was pink with a rose on it and black lettering. I was going to bring them home and throw them out, but the woman next to me in line spoke.

"Oh, do you do readings?"

I mumbled, "Yes."

"I run a hairdressing business," she said. "I'll send you clients!"

She did, and I'm still in that line of work. My awareness of intuition is that if we follow the prompts, the universe supports.

—Cyndi Dale

· · · · · · — · · · · · ·
PONDER THIS
IGNORING THE MESSAGE

When we listen to what our intuition is telling us, we will almost certainly benefit in some way. Alternatively, if we ignore the clairaudient messages we hear, we may miss out on something fantastic. Can you remember a time when you thought you heard something? How did you respond to it? Did you believe it was an intuitive impression? Did you listen to the message, or did you ignore it? Do you remember if there were consequences? You may be nervous or unsure about listening to what your clairaudience is telling you—especially if it's something potentially life-changing, like in Cyndi's story—but oh, the outcome can be magical!

Adriana

My client Adriana told me the moments she feels her intuition most strongly are when she ignores it. She confided that it took her many years to learn to trust the voice that was always trying to speak to her and keep her safe.

When Adriana was in her twenties, she was young, unemployed, and reckless. Her intuition tried to steer her away from ill-fated matches and haphazard decisions—not that she listened. She was kind of a rebel, and she acted out accordingly. In general, Adriana ignored her intuitive nudges; more specifically, she resisted her clairaudient orders. Adriana refused to listen to anyone, whether it was a friend, a stranger, or her own intuition.

One day, when Adriana was out breaking into cars to steal what she could, her intuition screamed at her, *Don't do it. Not this one!*

As was usual back then, Adriana ignored this thought. In fact, she intentionally disregarded it. She didn't want to hear it—she had no desire to be told what to do. So, Adriana told the guidance in her head to shut up, broke into the car, and took off, thinking she'd gotten away with it yet again.

That afternoon, after Adriana had returned home, a SWAT team banged down her door. They were there to arrest her for breaking into that car. This was a low point that started a chain of events that would change Adriana's life: jail, rehab, prison, and finally, gratefully, recovery. It also inspired Adriana to start listening to and trusting her intuition.

Scarlett

Scarlett and her high school friends were feeling restless one night and decided to, in her words, "do something illegal and stupid." They drove their car onto the high school track because, well, why not?

After driving around the track a couple of times, Scarlett's friends talked about driving to the baseball field nearby. But, in the middle of their last lap around the track, Scarlett heard, *Get off!* She instantly got a really bad feeling and yelled that they needed to get off the track and leave right away.

At first, her friends teased her. They said she was being wimpy. Then Scarlett told them what she'd heard, but they just looked at her with questioning expressions on their faces.

"Guys, I'm telling you! My intuition is screaming at me that we need to leave, and we need to leave right now!"

Scarlett's friends finally listened to her, thinking she was crazy the whole time. But as soon as they pulled into the parking lot, they saw a police car coming down the street, right next to the track. Had it not been for that intuitive voice yelling in her ear, Scarlett and all of her friends would have gotten in serious trouble. Her friends owe her big time!

Tina

When Tina was in elementary school, she lived on a dead-end dirt road. The road was essentially one lane, a tree-wrapped, winding road with a blind corner. Tina, intuitive since birth, always knew when there was a car coming around the blind corner. Whenever Tina and her mom were about to drive around the blind corner, she'd warn her mom if there was oncoming traffic.

"Mom, there's a car coming," she'd say.

"Honey, I don't see anything," her mother would respond.

"I'm telling you—there's a car coming!"

And sure enough, she'd be right. Tina always said she could hear the cars, though her mother never did. Eventually, they both realized Tina was intuitively hearing the cars. Even though her mom couldn't hear or see the cars, she knew her daughter had something special going on, so she paid attention to her when they were on the road.

Teresa

Teresa's boyfriend taught her how to ride a motorcycle. When she was on her bike, she felt great—she was living her best life! The couple loved driving together, side-by-side; it made Teresa feel very comfortable. After they broke up, Teresa figured she would keep riding without her boyfriend. She kind of wanted to prove she could do it. She would show him!

To fully commit to riding on her own, Teresa decided to sign up for a long group ride with four other people. She ended up leading the ride after the others unofficially nominated her as their front-runner. Teresa didn't feel so good about this—she didn't want to be the leader. It was the first time she'd ever led a ride, and her intuition was telling her it was not a good idea. She even heard *No!* as she started up her bike. As she was getting ready to take off, she heard *Stop!* Teresa knew this was her intuitive voice shouting at her, but she figured she was just being overly cautious because she was nervous without her ex-boyfriend riding next to her.

Unfortunately, Teresa dropped her bike right as the group was getting started. She should have stopped there. But, stubbornly, she didn't—she wanted to prove to herself and to her ex that she was fine without him. Again, she heard *No!* and ignored it.

Teresa got back on her bike, and the group rode on. They all agreed they would stop and get some lunch at a restaurant they would be riding past. While they ate, the group shared some laughter and good conversation. As they were getting ready to head back out, the group, once again, nominated Teresa to lead. She hemmed and hawed a bit but didn't argue too much—after all, it was kind of flattering. When she heard *Stop!* again, Teresa wrote it off, believing it was just her fear of doing this alone.

When it was time to leave, Teresa realized she couldn't find her keys. She worried it was a sign that went along with all of her clairaudient messages. The group looked everywhere and finally found them back in the restaurant, hidden by their dirty dishes. It was yet another universal warning that Teresa needed to stop driving, but she was committed, and she wasn't giving up.

As they took off, Teresa heard *No!* for the last time. She was becoming more and more uneasy; she had a nagging feeling that she was heading into something bad, but her ego kept her going.

The group was traveling uphill and turning a corner. The next thing Teresa knew, she was waking up in a helicopter. Apparently, she had ended up in a ravine; no one quite knew how, but her bike had skidded off the road.

The police and ambulance had come, called by the other riders, and they determined that a life support helicopter was necessary. The helicopter immediately brought her to a trauma center. A short time later, Teresa was in a cervical collar. Bruises covered almost her entire body, and she had a Grade 2 concussion. She was also diagnosed with traumatic shock. Thankfully, Teresa survived her injuries, but she never got on a motorcycle again.

In Teresa's words: "It seemed I should've listened to my intuition." But, all too often, our egos get in the way. We may ignore what our intuition is telling us because we have something to prove, either to ourselves or to someone else. Occasionally, we get lucky and our ego aligns with our intuition. But, when it doesn't and we discount our intuitive messages, there's usually some kind of consequence.

If you have a clairaudient experience and the message you hear goes against what you want or what you're doing, take a moment to decipher if it is your intuition or your ego talking. If it's your ego talking, is it holding you back or moving you forward? Most of the time, it will serve you better to check your ego at the door.

EXERCISE Hearing What You Want

It can be tough to determine whether a message is your ego or true clairaudience. So, for the purpose of this exercise, you're going to hear both.

Read the following statements with the expectation that you are going to answer from a place of want—meaning what you want the answer to be. As you read each question, let yourself hear the answer you desire:

+ Should you change your career?
+ Are you likable?
+ Should you look for a different job in your current profession?
+ Is your relationship a good one for you?
+ Will you make more friends soon?
+ Are you a good person?
+ Should you get a pet?
+ Do you need to change your exercise routine?

When you are all done, read each question again, this time allowing your clairaudience to respond instead; you may hear the answers in sounds or music or even words. When you are done, compare the answers from your ego to the answers from your clairaudience. How different were they? Did you hear the responses in different ways?

The questions you can ask are endless. The important thing is to decipher the difference between how your ego sounds and how your clairaudience sounds. Was your ego more negative?

Positive? Angry or happy? Did it make you doubt yourself? Keep practicing this skill by trying this exercise next time you are unsure of your direction.

Joseph

Joseph was in the Marines. When he was injured during active duty, he was taken to a hospital that served all of the military branches. He was in a large room with many different servicemen, but no one he knew. He missed his platoon brothers and sisters. Even though Joseph was surrounded by people, he still felt alone. This left him with nothing to do but think.

One day, while lying in bed recuperating, Joseph started hearing the sounds of battle. He heard gunshots and mortars, clear as day, but when he looked around, he saw none of the usual chaos of battle. None of the staff or patients were standing at attention or shouting orders or hiding. In fact, they were not showing any signs of hearing an attack.

Joseph called over the closest nurse.

"What is going on? Do you hear that?" he yelled.

"What are you talking about?" the nurse replied.

"Oh my god! Do you not hear the explosions outside?" he shouted.

By now, Joseph was feeling kind of crazy. He could still hear the battle, but no one else was responding. He knew they didn't hear it, but he had no idea *why* they couldn't. It made no sense. The noise was so loud he could barely hear himself talk.

The nurse called a doctor over and said, "He's acting irrationally. I'm worried he's suffering a traumatic episode."

The doctor picked up the chart at the end of the bed right as Joseph heard another burst of gunshots.

"How are we feeling today, Joseph?" the doctor asked.

"Well, *we* would be feeling a lot better if you all would get battle ready—I need a gun!" he insisted.

The doctor and nurse just stood there at looked at him.

"Joseph, you're okay. Do you know where you are and why you're here?"

"Yes, I'm no fool! But I need a gun!" he repeated.

As if in a bad movie, everything slowed down as Joseph realized the battle was being waged, but not yet. He was hearing what was coming, and that gave him a few minutes to prepare.

Joseph said, "Listen to me right now. I know you don't believe me. But my intuition is telling me it's coming. It is not—and I repeat, *not*—a drill. I am not in the middle of an episode; this is what's coming. Now please, someone get me a gun, and the rest of you, prepare to arm yourselves. The battle will be here in a few minutes. Just listen to me! If nothing happens by then, I will give you the gun back!"

This time, the hospital staff listened. They didn't quite believe Joseph, but they'd seen and heard a lot in this particular hospital. Against all odds, Joseph was right: the battle was coming to them. Within minutes, they all heard gunshots—there was no doubt. Thankfully, the gunshots only lasted for a couple of minutes; the enemy was kept outside of the hospital and never breached the doors.

After things calmed down, the staff looked at Joseph in shock.

"Yeah, I know. Sometimes I have intuitive messages. Usually it's not about the future, but obviously this time it was. I heard it almost the same way it actually just happened," he told them.

Precognitive intuition is when we experience something that hasn't happened yet. It's typically a precursor to an event. Joseph's intuitive awareness was probably amped up by the fact that he was in an almost meditative state, with his mind fully open to his thoughts, which allowed his intuition to come through.

Jared

There's an old saying in law enforcement: "Every cop is entitled to one mistake." This, apparently, is something every rookie learns; it serves as a warning, and also a cautionary tale. Jared, a rookie at the time, heard the words in his head over and over again as he made a routine traffic stop.

It was the middle of the night. Jared had just pulled over a vehicle in an area that had no streetlamps. He called the stop in on his radio, then got out of his car, making sure to have his gun holstered and his flashlight bright. As he cautiously walked up to the car, he had a nagging thought that most cars out at this time of night weren't up to anything good.

"Hi, officer. What's up?" the driver asked.

A quick peek inside the dark car showed Jared there were no passengers. He looked back and answered, "You were speeding—doing fifty in a thirty-five miles per hour zone. I'm going to need your license and registration, please."

"Sure. No problem, sir," the man responded, saccharine sweet.

Jared was familiar with the way people responded when they were pulled over. They tended to either be super sweet, cry and be very upset, or argue with you. This attitude was nothing out of the ordinary; fake sweetness was pretty standard for these late-night stops.

As the man reached for the glove compartment to retrieve the necessary documents, Jared shined his flashlight into the rear of the car. He was checking for anyone who may be hiding or in distress of some kind, or any weapons, drugs, or other contraband.

Suddenly, he heard, clairaudiently, another thing cops are always taught: *Always watch the hands!* Jared immediately thought, *Uh-oh!*

He looked into the front seat at the driver's hands. He was surprised to see the driver was actually reaching for a gun. The rest is history. Jared told the driver to get out of the car and lie face down on the ground. To this day, Jared feels he saved his own life by listening to his clairaudient messages.

A seasoned police officer once shared with me that he didn't really know whether he was using his training or his intuition on the job. This makes perfect sense, as cops have to use their instincts, and after all, listening to your intuition is instinctual!

Charlie

Officers often have other duties such as traffic control or construction redirection. Charlie, a police officer, was standing on the side of a road, directing traffic while workers were doing some underground pipe work on the street. He'd had a long day. Over six hours had gone by, and dusk was rapidly approaching.

Charlie's walkie-talkie was on his shoulder clip. He'd been half-heartedly listening to the various police station announcements throughout the day. Then, he heard a radio broadcast that stood out to him: a particular vehicle had just committed a street robbery, and there were shots fired—the perpetrators were armed and dangerous.

Now, this was not an uncommon dispatch. But what made Charlie pay attention was that his mind told him to keep his eyes peeled because he would see the vehicle soon. Charlie didn't question his intuition. Instead, he told the guys working that they should take a quick break because he needed to leave in a minute or two.

Sure enough, shortly after the dispatch came through, he saw the vehicle. He got into his police car and started following it. He couldn't approach it alone—he knew this—so he called for backup, knowing from prior experience that backup would take time to arrive. The car started heading for the highway and Charlie heard, clairaudiently, that it had to be stopped prior to getting on the interstate.

With a bit of apprehension, Charlie went ahead and stopped the car. He drew his weapon, remembering that the occupants were armed and dangerous, and quickly glanced into the front and back of the vehicle. He ordered the two occupants, the only people he'd seen, out of the vehicle and made them lie face down with their hands behind their backs. As they were doing that, backup arrived. Charlie briefly explained what was going on.

All of a sudden, Charlie heard *Are you sure?* clairaudiently. While backup monitored the two perpetrators, he returned to the vehicle to look around more thoroughly. It was then that he found a third sub-ject lying on the backseat with a MAC-10 machine pistol, shaking and scared, but ready to use the weapon if needed.

Charlie yelled, "Put it down, now!"

The third perpetrator put the weapon down, then got out and followed suit by lying on the ground. He was cuffed, along with his two buddies. The police found the stolen property in the trunk and arrested all three of them.

Fortunately, Charlie listened to his intuition both times: he knew he was going to see the car and, maybe more importantly, he knew to look in the back seat again. Charlie's clairaudience saved him and perhaps others. There are some cops who don't believe in intuition. There are also those who admit that their instincts are partly due to training, but also very attributable to intuitive gifts. Regardless of what they call it, their intuition can and does save lives.

Fran

Intuition can also serve us when we are being bamboozled. One winter, Fran and her husband were visiting New York City to do Christmassy things. They had taken the train into Grand Central and walked to Times Square to look at all of the decorations. They also went to Broadway to see a play.

After Times Square and the play, Fran and her husband stopped to eat. They had a nice, leisurely dinner, enjoying their time together. When they were getting ready to leave, they realized it was raining. They could either walk back to Grand Central in freezing cold rain, or they could hail a taxi. Even though the couple had never hailed a taxi in New York City before, the choice was easy: they would take a cab back.

Once in the cab, Fran and her husband relaxed in the back seat, pointing out a variety of touristy attractions as they drove back that they thought they may want to plan another trip into the city to check out. Then, the taxi pulled over in a dark, back alley.

"Here you are," the driver said to them.

Fran and her husband looked at each other. Even though Fran could hear cars honking and beeping, when she looked around, she didn't see any cars. She heard the noise again and realized her clairaudience was trying to tell her something.

Fran said, "We said Grand Central."

"Yes, yes, you're here!" the driver replied.

Again, Fran heard the horns blasting and she looked at her husband. She said, "No way. This is totally wrong."

He whispered to Fran, "Come on, let's just go. I don't want anything to happen."

Fran said to the driver, "This is absolutely not the entrance to Grand Central. I don't know what you're trying to pull, but we're not stupid."

"All you have to do is follow this sidewalk to the entrance. You can't get in the other way."

Fran's husband eyes pleaded with her to just get out. So, she acquiesced, even though she was still hearing car horns blasting in her mind. She cautiously got out of the cab, trusting her intuition was trying to warn her. It was a terrible spot—the sidewalk the driver had pointed out was merely a curb on the side of a huge cement wall, and cars suddenly swarmed around them. Luckily, Fran and her husband made it up onto the curb. Carefully, with their backs against the wall, they made their way around to the front.

It turned out the pair was at Grand Central, but they were at the back, which was dangerous and tunnellike. It would have been so simple for the driver to just drop them at the entrance, but he hadn't wanted to, probably because he'd have gotten stuck in the traffic there. The alley he'd dropped them off in was a straight shot back to the action—sans traffic, which meant more fares.

Fran told her husband, "Next time, listen to my intuition. I knew he was playing us."

He nodded his head, fully aware she'd been right.

Mercifully, not everyone gets clairaudient messages that are unfavorable. Now and again, we do get positive communications, because clairaudience is not just about negativity. Regardless, there are many positive outcomes when we pay attention to intuition.

· · · · · · — · · · · · ·

PONDER THIS
LISTENING FOR CLARITY

As with all intuitive messages, you may be aware of more than one meaning to what you're hearing. When you're dealing with clairaudient messages, what you hear may excite you or scare you—or both at the same time!—so pay attention to your other gifts as well. Let your helper senses assist you; they can help you translate what your clairaudient message actually means.

For example, how do you feel when you hear your message? Do you see anything along with the sound? If you still can't determine what the message actually means, ask for another message. There's nothing wrong with asking for clarity, and when you do, you just might find that your initial impression was spot-on.

Laurel

Laurel had what she called a "birth announcement" clairaudient experience, though she had no idea that was what it was until afterward! One day, while working from home, Laurel heard, *Call Jeff*. Jeff was one of Laurel's coworkers. He and his wife were expecting a baby. Laurel's intuitive nudge was a happy one, so without a second thought, she picked up the phone.

As she was waiting for Jeff to answer, Laurel began to worry that something was wrong—she didn't want to interrupt if something wasn't going right. Laurel did her best to stay positive and left a message for Jeff to call her back as soon as he could. She told him it was not about work, but she wanted to know if everything was okay with the baby. After hanging up, Laurel heard, *He will call*, though she was still a little worried.

The next morning, Jeff called her back. "What the heck?" he asked. "Do you have a sixth sense or something?"

"Oh no … Is everything okay?" she asked. She felt tears beginning to appear in her eyes.

Jeff responded, "We just had the baby! How did you know?"

"Oh, I'm so happy for you!" Laurel screeched, the sad tears turning into happy ones.

Jeff shared all the details. His wife had unexpectedly gone into labor three weeks early. Miraculously, their beautiful baby girl was healthy and even had a head of curly blond hair. Jeff and his wife were ecstatic. So was Laurel. This story demonstrates that there are positive clairaudient messages to be heard as well as the warnings.

Stephanie and Rose

One day Stephanie and her daughter, Rose, were walking through a parking lot on their way into a home goods store. They both heard a little boy mumbling "My mommy!" as he ran out of the store and into the parking lot.

Other people just ignored him, probably believing he was following his mother, as a few women had exited the store right before him. This would have made perfect sense, but Stephanie and Rose stopped. At the same time, they internally heard horns blasting and the boy crying. They looked at each other and, without hesitation, turned around and began walking in the direction the boy had just gone. He had almost made it to the end of the parking lot and into traffic; the boy was spinning and mumbling. Stephanie and Rose looked at each other, collectively heard *Help him*, and instinctively knew what they had to do. They went up to him and gently asked if he knew where his mommy was.

"No," he practically whispered, clearly afraid.

Stephanie heard with her intuitive ears, *Inside*. She knew that meant they needed to bring the boy back inside the store; she presumed he had lost track of his mom and run outside looking for her. Stephanie knew the boy would be afraid to hold her hand, so she asked if he could hold on to a shopping cart. She explained she wanted to keep him safe because it was a big, scary parking lot with lots of cars pulling in and out. As they started moving, she slowly put her hand over his, and he looked up at her and gave her a slight smile.

When they entered the store, Stephanie and Rose were expecting to hear a woman shouting and looking for her son. Instead, they heard nothing. The little boy couldn't have been more than four years old, yet here he was with two strangers; clearly, no one was missing him. So, the pair tried another tactic.

"What's your mommy's name?" Stephanie asked him.

"Mommy," the boy replied.

With a chuckle, Rose jumped in and asked, "What do other people call her?"

He answered, "Carmen."

Stephanie and Rose began yelling for Carmen throughout the store. She responded and was reunited with her son. Stephanie and Rose knew their intuition had led them to help the boy, possibly saving him from a serious accident in the parking lot.

Carrie

Carrie had recently moved to a new state six hours from home. She'd had a psychiatrist where she used to live, and she took medicine that was prescribed by that psychiatrist. She realized, a little too late, that she was almost out of her meds—she only had four pills left in the ninety-day bottle. Needing a medication refill hadn't crossed her mind during the moving process; she had so many other things going on that she forgot to look for a new doctor.

Carrie started to panic once she realized her medication was about to run out. She didn't know what to do: she couldn't see that psychiatrist anymore—there was no way she was going to drive twelve hours round-trip to get her medicine—but she didn't know what other choice she had. She would have to wait months to get an appointment with a new psychiatrist in her area.

Suddenly, Carrie heard, *There is a better way. There is a different way.* She couldn't figure out what it meant. She knew the medicine she needed was prescription-only; she couldn't just walk into a pharmacy and get something over the counter to replace it. As she was worrying about her options, she heard again, *There is a better way. There is a different way.*

Carrie wondered if she was going crazy, which didn't make her feel any better about the situation. Then she heard *Telemedicine!* She hadn't even considered that. She reached out to her old psychiatrist, who assured Carrie she could squeeze her in, and they had a telemed session that morning. After their session, Carrie's doctor was able to send a refill prescription to her new pharmacy.

Carrie was glad she had listened to her intuition instead of panicking. Although her situation was not immediately life-threatening, it would have been a definite problem for her. Clairaudient impressions can show up to help us in all sorts of situations.

EXERCISE Ask for Help

Sometimes hearing a few words can really help us make a decision. Think of a question you have; it could be about something important, or it could be something you're just curious about. Then, say aloud (or in your mind), "I wish to know about …" and fill in what you are questioning.

Wait for an answer to come. Allow it to come through with just a couple of words.

Once you hear an answer, ask for validation. This time, allow it to come through in any form of clairaudience: sounds, words, names, song lyrics, etc. It doesn't matter how the message shows up this time—just allow it to speak to you!

Did the second answer validate the first answer? Or was it totally different? Either way, you can ask for more clarification if you need it. Allow your clairaudient messages to help you interpret an answer to your question.

Listen Up

When I do readings and the person doesn't resonate with what I'm telling them, more often than not, it's because it hasn't happened yet. I tell my clients at the beginning of a session that I read the past, the present, and the future, and it's possible that if they don't understand what I'm talking about, it may make sense in three months (or three days).

The same goes for us as readers. We may not recognize what we're hearing or what we're receiving intuitively, but that doesn't mean we should discount it. File every message away in your memory; someday, that message may help you in a situation, or it may help you understand something.

Remember that clairaudient messages are those that you hear. It doesn't matter if your intuition shows up as a word, a sound, or music playing; however you receive your clairaudient messages is okay. They are a valid (and sometimes loud) message just for you. Many people think being clairaudient means you are able to have full-on conversations with your intuition, but that's generally not how it works. Instead, pay attention to all the other ways clairaudience may appear in your life—listen up!

PRO TIP

Clairaudient messages can be sounds, music, song lyrics, and even words.

Chapter 6

CLAIRGUSTANCE AND CLAIRALIENCE

Sometimes our intuition relays messages via taste or smell. If you've experienced a fleeting moment that had you questioning whether what you just sensed was your imagination, this may have been clairgustance (clear taste) and clairalience/clairolfaction (clear smell).

Connected Clairs

You may overlook these intuitive messages; it can be difficult to know if you're just getting a whiff of something or someone nearby. One tip for identifying clairgustance and clairolfaction is that these intuitive senses are often experienced together, similar to our physical senses of taste and smell.

Kristy Robinett

Kristy Robinett is a psychic medium and author of many books, including *Embrace Your Empathy*. She occasionally experiences clairgustance and clairalience. One such experience happened when she and her husband were picking up concert tickets for a future event. As they waited in line, Kristy noticed the woman in front of her had a very scattered physical and psychic energy—so much so that she ended up hitting Kristy in the face with her purse as she agitatedly swung around.

The woman was ashamed and apologetic. Kristy accepted her apology and then noticed her stomach was growling. She turned to her husband and told him she wanted to get German food, even mentioning schnitzel, sauerkraut, and Bratkartoffeln. Kristy's husband thought that was strange, as they never ate German food, but the woman in front of Kristy knew exactly what they were talking about and said as much. After they got their tickets and left, Kristy was still hungry but didn't remember talking about German food.

A few weeks later, we were back at the concert hall for the show, and as two women squeezed in, one stepped on my foot. She plopped down in her seat, ungracefully took her coat off (hitting me in the side of the head while doing so), and leaned over to apologize. It was the same lady who had hit me with her purse when we were getting the tickets! Her eyes widened and she began to cry. I was horrified: *What did I do?* The woman elbowed her sister, pointed at me, and began to cry harder.

Apparently, the day we picked up the tickets, her sister had received a call that their grandmother passed away that morning. Their grandma was German and lived in Germany. They often spent their summer vacations with her, and she would inundate them with the German culture. When the woman had heard me mention German food in line that day, she was shocked.

"I think it must've been a heaven hello," I said gently, not wanting to tell them what I did for a living but offering validation nonetheless. "She was probably trying to assure you she made it to the other side and was celebrating with fried potatoes."

—Kristy Robinett

Kristy was able to bring the sisters some comfort that day. If they had not crossed paths again, Kristy would never have understood where her sudden craving for German food came from. She was grateful she was able to put two and two together after the fact. Prior to that experience, Kristy's clairgustance and clairolfaction had never picked up on German flavors—a pleasant surprise!

Christine

If your intuition shows up via clairgustance and clairalience, there will absolutely be times that you'll taste or smell something pretty nasty. Other times, you may find yourself tasting a flavor you enjoy—that is much better than tasting something you don't! Tasting or smelling something good may guide you to do something you hadn't planned to do, which is what happened to Christine one Friday night.

Christine, a psychotherapist, was talking with her husband about what they wanted to eat that night, as well as what they wanted to drink.

"Well, this is interesting. I'm tasting sangria. I don't know why. I wasn't planning on making it," Christine said.

"Do you want to go out and get some?" her husband asked. He thought they were in for a night at a Mexican restaurant.

"No, I think I need to make it..." she mused, almost to herself. In the past, Christine had made sangria, but only if she had open wine bottles and fruit that was on the brink of going bad—neither of which they had at the moment. However, something was telling her to make sangria. She could taste it.

As she started pulling together ingredients, her husband said, "Why are you going to open a new bottle? And all that fruit is something we can just eat. Are you sure you want to waste it? We don't even have any leftover alcohol." He was the kind of guy that made delicious things out of food that was about to spoil. In this situation, his wife using all-new ingredients felt wasteful.

Ignoring his questions and protests, Christine proceeded to open a new bottle of wine. And, to add insult to injury, she also opened a new bottle of Grand Marnier and a new bottle of vodka.

Knowing it was better to just go along at this point, her husband asked, "When are we going to drink the sangria?"

She told him it wouldn't be ready until Sunday.

"Well, then why did you make it?"

"Because I tasted it and felt I was supposed to."

Now, Christine was no stranger to psychic abilities and intuition. However, she usually didn't experience clairgustance or clairalience. For some reason, though, she felt it was important to adhere to this intuitive direction.

And she was right. The next day, Christine received a last-minute invitation to a therapist gathering on Sunday; she knew a few of the therapists invited, but most she didn't. As she debated whether or not to go, a colleague messaged her to say the gathering was going to have a Mexican theme and asked if Christine could bring some drinks. Her sangria would be ready at the perfect time! If she didn't already have sangria made, she probably wouldn't have gone. Luckily, she'd paid attention to her intuition. Christine went to the gathering and ended up having a great time, and her sangria was a hit.

EXERCISE Taste Your Answer

You can use your clairgustance to determine whether something is positive or negative. In other words, you can get an answer to your question using your intuitive taste. The best way to do this is to qualify different tastes. The following tastes will allow you to decipher whether something will have a more- or less-favorable outcome.

Take a second to move your tongue around inside your mouth, getting to know what it tastes like already. Then, go ahead and interpret the following flavors, allowing them to evoke a yes, a no, or even a neutral connotation:

Tomato sauce	Garbage
Ice cream	Alcohol
Cigarettes	Soda
Ginger	Hot sauce
Hamburgers	Corn
Pineapple	Dirt
Salt water	Pretzels
Chocolate cake	Salt
Pepper	Salad dressing
Fish	Bananas
Chicken	Coconut
Oranges	Peas
Lemon	Beer
Ghost peppers	Refried beans
Coffee	Lip gloss
Fried rice	Pizza

As you can see, the list can go on and on. However, these basic flavors should give you some indication of which way your intuition leans. For example, I don't have much of a spice tolerance, so the mere thought of tasting a ghost pepper would make me run! That one obviously evokes a negative response for me.

Did you have more positive than negative responses? Did any flavors make you think of someone or something? There's no limit to how you may interpret the flavors.

Laurence

Unfortunately, not every experience with clairgustance or clairalience has a positive outcome. Laurence had one such occasion while visiting his father in their childhood home. Laurence had moved to New York a few years prior and was happy to be back in Connecticut. Since they lived about six hours apart, Laurence and his dad were excited to spend some quality time together.

They spent the first day just enjoying each other's company, talking about Laurence's kids and how he was enjoying the new place in New York. He shared that he wished his dad was there with them.

"Well, I'm retired now, so you never know. Maybe I will consider it," his dad told him.

As the two talked, they realized there really wasn't anything keeping Laurence's dad from moving. They had no other living family, and since he'd recently retired, he was free and clear to sell his house and move.

"Wow! Let's do this," Laurence said, excited.

They immediately looked up other houses for sale in the neighborhood, and Laurence realized his father's home was worth a lot more money than they'd expected. He reached out to an old friend

who was a realtor, and she came over that evening to do an evalua-
tion. As they were walking through the house, Laurence unexpectedly smelled cigarette smoke.

"Dad, are you smoking again?" he asked.

"Nope! Haven't smoked in a year. Why?"

"I don't know. I just smelled cigarette smoke really strongly."

The realtor chimed in that she didn't smoke, so it wasn't her.

The three of them finished walking through the house, and his
dad decided to list it with the realtor. Suddenly, Laurence smelled
cigarettes again. He thought that maybe someone outside was smoking, so he ignored it.

That night while Laurence and his father had dinner together,
they talked about the upcoming move. They were debating whether
Laurence's father should buy a place in New York or move in with
Laurence and his family for a bit first. Out of the blue, Laurence
smelled his mother's perfume. He told his dad, and the two took it as
confirmation that he should move into Laurence's basement, as there
was a private entrance, and it would be perfect for an in-law suite.

Things moved quickly after that. The realtor sold the house
within a week, and Laurence arranged the move. A month and a half
later, Laurence's dad was all settled in. One day, Laurence smelled
cigarette smoke again, and he tasted what he could only describe as
decay. It was then that everything clicked—an intuitive aha moment.
Laurence told his dad that he needed to go to the doctor right away,
and they made an appointment for the next day.

Unfortunately, after running some tests, Laurence's father was
diagnosed with stage 4 throat cancer. He'd had flu-like symptoms, a
cough, and a sore throat for a while but hadn't thought anything of
it. The cigarette smoke Laurence had been smelling was his intuition
trying to let him know that his dad was dying from cancer, likely a

result of his many years as a smoker. Laurence is convinced that his intuitive messages came from the other side: they were his mother's way of trying to prepare him for what was coming.

Ultimately, moving to Laurence's house gave the father and son almost a year together before his dad passed. They felt so blessed to have that time together.

Laurence's parents are still conspiring to send him intuitive messages. As with all the intuitive nudges, messages present themselves in a variety of ways and for a multitude of reasons. These messages may be positive or negative, they may influence or inform, or they may just be a hello from heaven.

EXERCISE Smelling Illness

Illnesses can often be smelled with our physical sense. They might also be smelled with a psychic sense. This exercise will help provide some guidelines for clairaliently deciphering scents around people.

To begin, clear your mind and take a deep breath. Let your imagination lead you as you experience the following scents. You can add to the meanings I've shared or even change them, as your interpretations may be different than mine.

- **Decay:** Can represent that someone very ill is nearing the end of their life; specifically, someone who has a tumor or cancer eating away at them

- **Burning, Smoldering, or Heat:** May indicate someone's joint cushioning or cartilage is weakening or wearing away

- **Septic Smell on Breath:** Digestive issues or unhealthy stomach

+ **Rotting Smell on Breath:** Cavity or issues with teeth
+ **Sweaty Smell or Garbage Smell:** Bad diet
+ **Copper Scent:** Heart or blood issues

These are some of the scents you may intuitively smell on someone who is ill, regardless of their physical scent. As with all of your intuitive gifts, please be thoughtful about sharing your impressions with other people, specifically if you think you detect illness, as you could be incorrect, especially if you are not practiced.

Remember that these scents are just a few of the many you may need to intuitively interpret. In fact, you may notice over time that you have your own telltale odors that routinely pop up.

Nikki

Nikki was the manager of a local coffee shop and bakery. She had quite a few customers who came in and chatted with her while waiting for their order. Customers liked Nikki and enjoyed stopping by the bakery for its delicious goodies as well as the great service they received. Not all of the bakery's customers were regulars, though. One non-regular came in and ordered a few loaves of bread and a coffee, then left after sharing that she was headed to the organic market, the wine and cheese shop, and the salon and spa, all in the same plaza.

"Okay, enjoy your day," Nikki said. She thought coffee shop employees were like therapists at times—people felt very comfortable sharing with them.

Nikki went about the rest of her day. She locked up alone, after the kitchen and front staff left, and was counting out the cash drawer when she heard a loud bang on the shop's door. When Nikki looked up, she was startled to see the customer from earlier.

I hope there wasn't anything wrong with her order, Nikki thought as she made her way to the front of the shop. After she unlocked and opened the door, she said, "Hi. I'm sorry, we're closed. Is there something you need?"

"I'm sorry to bother you. I'm just wondering if you found any keys? I can't seem to find mine anywhere, and I'm retracing my steps," the woman responded.

"Let me take a peek," Nikki replied, letting the woman come in and look as well.

The two searched on every surface and even looked underneath the display cases and tables to make sure the keys hadn't fallen behind or under something.

"I'm sorry. It doesn't seem like they are here. Have you checked at the other shops?" Nikki asked.

The woman said she would go look. Nikki locked the door behind her and was busy finishing up the closing procedures when she got a strong whiff of garbage. She looked around the shop and couldn't find the source; the smell was gone as quickly as it had come.

Nikki was just turning off the lights when the customer came back and knocked on the door again.

"I'm sorry, but I didn't find them. Did you, by chance?" the woman asked.

"No, I'm sorry, I haven't," Nikki answered. As soon as the words were out of her mouth, she smelled a strong scent of garbage again.

"Ugh. It's going to cost about four hundred dollars to replace them, minimum. I lost the other set, and this is the only key I have left," the woman said. "But thanks for your help!"

"Hold on a second," Nikki said. "Come with me, outside." She led the woman over to the dumpster, which thankfully was not full yet, and found the bag of trash that she'd taken out of the shop. Nikki took out the bag and opened it up. Right there, near the top, was a set of car keys.

"Oh, my goodness—how did you know?" the woman exclaimed.

"I smelled them," she said with a laugh as the customer looked at her in confusion and gratitude.

They both went back into the shop to wash their hands. When she was finished, the woman handed Nikki a fifty-dollar bill.

"You have no idea how much aggravation you've saved me. I appreciate all you did, especially going into the dumpster for me!" she said.

What a day, Nikki thought as she finished locking up and got in her car, fifty dollars richer. She knew her intuitive senses had saved the day—she just hoped that next time wouldn't involve dumpster diving.

Kristy Robinett

It would be wonderful if all we tasted, intuitively, was deliciousness: chocolate, ice cream, cake, or even a delicious meal. But quite often, we taste things we don't like: cigars or cigarettes, chemicals, or even garbage. The good news is that the sense will go away. As long as you recognize it for what it is, and discern what it means, you won't have to suffer for long.

Kristy, the psychic, author, and healer mentioned earlier in this chapter, once had a session where she kept tasting chili. She mentioned it to her client, although she thought she may just be hungry. The client revealed that his grandfather had won numerous chili competitions and had taken his famous recipe to the grave. Or had he?

Kristy said, "Your grandfather just whispered the secret ingredient to me. He told me I could give you the secret ingredient, but only if you start doing chili competitions yourself!"

His grandson, her client, agreed, and he has been winning chili competitions ever since.

Kristy's clairgustance worked hand-in-hand with her natural psychic and medium abilities. Recognizing what she was tasting further enhanced the moment and helped her client recognize his deceased relative was coming through. Bonus: she was able to taste his award-winning chili!

Kristy is a professional, but as you've probably realized by now, professionals like Kristy and I are not the only ones who have clairgustant or clairalient impressions. These intuitive senses may not be very common, but they do show up—sometimes at very spicy times.

Daisy

It took Daisy quite a while to figure out what was happening when she kept tasting what she could only describe as ghost pepper. She had decided to open a new store and was looking for a business partner. Her sights were set on Celia. Celia had experience in ownership, as she had opened three other stores previously, so Daisy was very excited about this potential venture.

When they first started discussing the possibility, they were out having drinks. Daisy suddenly spit her drink out.

"What's going on?" Celia asked her.

"I don't know! I just tasted something super spicy. I don't do spicy," Daisy answered. She was drinking a margarita, and she wondered if the server had given her a spicy margarita instead of a plain one.

Celia and Daisy kept talking, this time about family and vacations. Then they talked about possible locations for their new store. Daisy took another sip of her drink and tasted the spice again. Not sure what was happening, she decided to ask their server for a new drink. This time, she ordered vodka with club soda and a slice of lime, knowing there should be nothing spicy in that.

The pair continued talking about other things, and Daisy's new drink came. Everything was fine. "It must have just been my drink," Daisy told Celia. She didn't have any spicy blasts the rest of the evening.

After they left, agreeing to talk the next day about the store opening, Daisy went home and told her husband what had happened.

"Well, that's interesting," he said.

"It must've just been a spicy margarita instead of a plain margarita," Daisy told him.

"Do you think it was your intuition?"

"What do you mean? That doesn't make sense."

They both let it go. The next day, Celia and Daisy were talking about opening the store and officially renting a space when Daisy got the same spicy taste. This time, the women were talking on the phone, and Daisy was just drinking a glass of water. But every sip she took while they talked tasted like a hot pepper. She told Celia she had to go because she wasn't feeling well.

That night, Daisy asked her husband what he thought.

"I think you need to think twice about this store. I believe it's your intuition telling you it's not a good idea. Maybe you need to listen to it. Use me as an excuse. Let Celia know you're sorry, but you just can't do it."

The next day, Daisy told Celia she had to back out. Luckily, they hadn't signed anything yet. She wished Celia nothing but the best and conveyed her apologies while making it clear that she was not going to move forward with her. Then, Daisy forgot all about it for about six months, never getting that spicy taste again.

In that time, Celia had gone ahead and opened the store with someone else. Then COVID happened, and the retail market was hit hard during the pandemic. Celia ended up declaring bankruptcy without telling her business partners, and her partners for that store and her others were left holding the bag for all of the business debt, including their leases on the properties.

Daisy had dodged a bullet. Fortunately, her husband had helped her interpret her own intuitive impressions. She had never experienced anything like that before, but now she realizes that every time she discussed opening the store, her intuition was conveying she should be cautious about the venture. It took her husband looking at it from a different perspective to expose what she needed to understand. Daisy knows that if she hadn't heeded the spicy warning, she'd be in a really bad place financially.

As with Daisy's clairgustance, your intuition can show up in a totally unexpected way. If you're not expecting it or aren't used to it informing you in this way, it can take a while to understand it. That doesn't negate what's happening. As for why Daisy got a spicy impression when she thought of going into business with Celia, some individuals carry their own specific taste or scent.

EXERCISE Smelling and Tasting People

While not always crucial, assigning a metaphysical taste or scent to people can be helpful, especially for future moments when you are trying to figure out who your intuition is sharing a message about.

Make sure you are by yourself, with no one else near you. As always, relax. Take a deep breath. Then go over the following list and allow yourself time to really smell or taste what each person or group of people presents as. You may get impressions of spices, flowers, cigarettes, coffee, salt water, etc. The possibilities are endless! Noting the impressions you get for the people in this list can help you decode your interpretations in the future.

Spouse or significant other	Daughter
Son	Father
Mother	Sibling
Astronaut	Salesman
Teacher	Boss
Coworker	Cashier
Chef	Baby
Debt collector	Best friend
Enemy	Doctor
Police officer	Firefighter
Waiter	Scientist

Did any of your answers surprise you? Did the impressions you tasted or smelled make sense? If you didn't experience something for all of them, that's all right. You can go back and try again, or you can wait and discover what you smell or taste when you're actually exposed to that person.

Tony

Sometimes what you smell or taste may be more about the type of person rather than the specific person, or it could be a combination of both. Tony learned that the hard way.

Tony and Ashley met one night at a bar and did shots together. It wasn't a big deal: they were both there, standing next to each other ordering drinks; they were both attractive and young and enjoyed each other's company. They danced a little, nothing slow, just fun and upbeat music. Tony was there with his friends and Ashley said she was with hers as well, but she asked if he would take her number so they could hang out again.

"Sure. This was fun," he told her.

The next day, Tony's friends came over to watch a game on TV. They all razzed him about his new girl, and when he told them he had her number, they all agreed he should call her. So, he did. Tony and Ashley chatted for a while and decided to meet up again in a couple of days.

As Tony told his buddies what the two of them had talked about, he started smelling something, something that he explained smelled like the worst gas anyone ever expelled. He yelled, "Woah! Who was that? You guys are rotten!"

Immediately, each of Tony's friends exclaimed it wasn't them. After having a little laugh, they continued watching the game.

Then one of the friends asked, "So where are you going with Ashley?"

Everyone in the room started oohing and ahhing, teasing Tony about his soon-to-be date.

"I'm supposed to meet her at the Ark. You know, that new restaurant on the water," Tony answered.

"Wow, you must really be into her if you're taking her there!" his friends cried.

"Woah, slow your roll! And—who the hell did it this time?" Tony shrieked, smelling the odor again. "You are rank!"

Again, everyone denied responsibility for stinking up the room.

"Well, it's one of you, and it is *bad*," Tony insisted.

They all looked at each other questioningly.

"I don't actually smell anything," one of them said. The rest of them nodded their heads in agreement.

"Well, it wasn't me," Tony replied, "but I don't smell it anymore."

They all sat back and finished watching the game. When Tony's friends were getting ready to leave, they razzed him once more about going out with Ashley. As they were doing so, Tony got a whiff of that same smell.

"Okay, this time I know it had to be one of you! You're nasty!" Tony bellowed. "Take your gross butts out of here!"

Two days went by, and Tony started thinking about his date that night. As he was thinking about Ashley, he smelled the same odor again, very briefly. He wondered if the culprit was actually his bathroom or the septic, not his friends. Just as quickly as he smelled the stench, it was gone—until he started getting ready to meet Ashley. The smell got so putrid he hurried out of his apartment.

On his way to the restaurant, Tony couldn't get rid of the smell. He figured it must have been stuck in his nose since it had been so bad before he left. He arrived at the restaurant and saw that Ashley was already seated. He got a super strong whiff of the sewer smell again, so much so that he asked the hostess if she smelled anything strange.

"No, why? Is everything okay?" she responded.

"Okay, that's weird. I just smelled something gross. But thanks," he told the hostess as they walked to the table where Ashley sat.

"Hi!" she said, standing to give him a quick hug in greeting.

The smell still lingered. Tony tried to ignore it, and they ordered drinks and appetizers. Then a gust of that smell hit him all over again. This time it was so strong he had to stand up and tell Ashley he was going to use the restroom. As he walked away, he saw a group of men, all in suits, rushing toward their table. They stopped in front of Ashley, and Tony heard them say, "Show us your hands! You are under arrest!"

As they shouted at her, she raised her hands and looked at Tony with a sad smile. She mouthed, "Sorry."

Tony got another overwhelming stench of sewage as they walked Ashley past him, handcuffs and all. It was in that moment he knew what the scent had been: every time he talked about her, and every time he thought of her, he was repulsed by a septic, gassy smell. He now understood the smell was his clairalience trying to warn him not to go out with her. And, to back up his newly discovered intuition, Tony soon learned that Ashley was wanted for murder in another state on the other side of the country, and she'd been hiding out for the last three months. She was trying to start over, and Tony knew he could have been her next victim. He was lucky that the FBI found her before it was too late.

Yum, Yum, Smells…Good?

It's never fun to smell something disgusting. I'd much rather smell flowers or candy than gas or garbage, but as you've read, these clairalient smells were there to help. Even the most unattractive odors may have a positive purpose.

Though clairgustance and clairalience are both uncommon ways for intuition to manifest, they do show up from time to time. You may smell something when trying to locate a missing item, like a sudden scent of soap if you left your phone in the laundry room. You may smell something that reminds you of a deceased loved one, a message sent from the other side to remind you they're around. Or maybe, if you're lucky, you'll run to the store to pick up the ice cream you just tasted with your clairgustance, and as you walk by the customer service desk, you'll decide to buy a winning lottery ticket.

PRO TIP

Pay attention to what you're doing, discussing, or thinking about when you suddenly taste or smell something—that may be key to discerning whether it's a moment of clairgustance or clairalience.

Chapter 7

SIGNS AND SYNCHRONICITIES

Signs are not the same thing as symbols, which I talked about earlier. Symbols are intuitive images, thoughts, or feelings that you have in your mind; they are internal messages that are untouchable. Signs, on the other hand, can be actually touched or seen externally, and they show up in a variety of ways.

Concrete Signs

Signs are a part of the intuitive family that is actually tangible.

Tammy Nelson

Dr. Tammy Nelson has plenty of experience working with signs. She is a world-renowned psychotherapist, TEDx speaker, and the author of multiple books, including *The New Monogamy*. She's been intuitive her entire life and uses her intuition when she works with clients as well as in her personal life:

I was working and living bicoastally, splitting my time each month between Connecticut and California. I had been doing this for over six months, and I knew I had to decide whether to pull the trigger and move to California full-time or not. It had been something I'd been pondering for a while, but I hadn't yet made a decision. My family was in Connecticut, and so was most of my practice. But, having been born in California, I'd always felt a pull to go back there—I felt a strong connection to the West Coast.

While in Santa Monica on the last day of the month before going home to Connecticut, I decided to go for a walk on the beach. Each step in the sand made me feel warm, but I still didn't know if it was meant for me to pack up and move clear across the country. I'd made my lists, but the pros and cons I'd written down still weren't answering my questions.

So, as I walked, I asked for a sign. I knew it had to be a big sign. It had to be in-my-face big or I wouldn't pay attention to it. I continued walking on the beach for about five more minutes. Then, I looked down and saw a huge heart drawn in the sand with my name smack in the middle of it. When I say huge, it was about ten feet across. It was exactly what I needed, and at that point I knew, without a doubt, that it was my sign to move to the beach!

—Tammy Nelson, PhD

Not all signs will be as big as the one Tammy had. It's not realistic to expect a bright light with an arrow pointing to the answer to our question. But, if we're lucky, we may recognize signs that will guide us to make a choice or a decision, or even let us know what's coming up. Signs are available to anyone who is willing to open themselves up to the possibility of their existence. They are put into our lives to help validate our intuition, and some people pay more attention to signs because of their actual physical existence. When our intuition sends us a sign that we can see, touch, or hear externally, it tends to be easier to identify.

· · · · · · — · · · · · ·

PONDER THIS
SIGNS

We've all experienced some kind of sign. Think back to one you've had. What was it? Did you acknowledge it immediately or, in retrospect, have you realized it was a sign that you ignored? Do you believe the sign was there to help you? Or was it trying to guide you to make a change?

Kim

When Kim and her husband first married, she wanted to have a baby with him; she already had three healthy, happy teenage children, but they wanted one together. Kim and her husband went to the doctor and were told he had no viable sperm. The fertility specialists told them there was no chance they would even get pregnant. After hearing this devastating news, Kim scheduled a reading with me, and I told her they would get pregnant in June but that she may not carry to term. In other words, she may not actually have another baby.

One night in June, Kim was driving home from a football game with her mom and her sons, and she saw a shooting star. At that moment, she knew she was pregnant. She didn't know how she knew, but she got a test and found out she was correct. She'd just known when she'd seen the shooting star.

When Kim was ten weeks pregnant, she and her husband went to get a sonogram. The baby measured appropriately, but there was no movement. The doctor ordered a more detailed sonogram. On their drive to that second sonogram, the song "Patience" by Guns N' Roses came on the radio. Kim knew at that moment that they were not going to get the outcome they wanted, and she told her husband that. Sure enough, she miscarried.

Kim also knew the song was a sign that she needed to be patient, but it was not one of her strong suits. Soon after, her husband became very sick, and more and more of Kim's time was spent caring for him. After a difficult battle, she lost him a few years later. Kim knows this experience would have been so much harder if she'd carried the pregnancy to term and had both a sick husband and a young child to care for.

Kim acknowledged two different signs: When she saw the shooting star, she knew without a doubt that she was pregnant. Then she heard the song, and again, she immediately knew it meant her pregnancy would not carry to term. While Kim was presented with signs prior to big life events, she acknowledges that signs can show up at the end of a process as well. Sometimes signs are the cherry on top, providing you with confirmation when you least expect it.

Ron

After Ron retired, he debated whether or not he should move. His family was scattered around the United States, so there wasn't one particular area he felt drawn to. The one thing he was sure of was his home had to remain the gathering place for his kids and their families, so he needed a house big enough for all of them—otherwise, he wasn't moving.

Ron decided to casually begin looking for a new place. He was open to living anywhere, but only if he found the perfect place. He looked online for a couple of months, but he wasn't seeing anything he loved, and he said as much while having coffee with a friend.

"I don't know, nothing stands out. I feel like it has to jump out at me or it's not meant to be," Ron told his good friend Casey.

Casey replied, "Ron, you'll know it when you see it. Wherever you go, your kids will visit. You don't have to worry about that. Just like this coffee called to me, you're like the island that beckons to them." Casey had ordered a special at the coffee shop; it was called "Chocolate Island"—a coffee with a chocolate truffle floating on top, surrounded by whipped cream. The two men laughed at the comparison.

Ron resumed looking for the perfect place. Another week went by, and he called his daughter to share his progress—or, as he put it, his non-progress.

"I don't know, Sandra. I'm not finding anything. I want somewhere that will be fun to visit but still feels like home. I want you and your brothers and my grandkids to enjoy coming to see me and not feel like it's a chore," he told her.

"Dad, of course we will visit. You know we love you. No matter where you are. It's not like you'll be stuck on a desert island or something. We will come to you!" she insisted. There was that word again: *island*.

Inspired by his daughter's reassurance, Ron continued looking. One day, he turned on the radio while he browsed, humming along to the song playing: "Islands in the Stream." His phone rang just then, and he answered it.

"How's it going, Dad?" his youngest son asked.

"I don't know. I feel like I'm just going to end up alone, all by myself, with no one visiting me," he answered.

"Oh Dad, don't say that. Even if you were on your own private island, we'd still come see you!" his son said.

The next day, Ron turned on the television. He flipped through the channels and stopped on HGTV. There was a show on that caught his eye: *Island Hunters*. While he watched, he opened his real estate app, and the first listing that appeared was for a house on an island off the coast of Washington state. It had easy access to the mainland and the location provided a change of seasons. Plus, the house looked absolutely perfect. Ron was cautiously optimistic. He contacted the realtor and booked a viewing for the following week.

It turned out the house *was* perfect. It had all the space Ron needed, plus the property had plenty of trees that his family could decorate for the holidays. Ron realized that he'd missed all of the signs—island references had been popping up the whole time he'd been looking!

Ron closed on his new home just in time for Christmas, and his whole family stayed for an entire week, all the way through New Year's Day. One evening, while they were sitting around watching a light snow fall, Ron recounted all of the times islands were mentioned during his housing search. His family agreed it was a sign that he hadn't quite picked up on at first, but they were sure glad he finally got the message.

Terry

When it comes to homes, not all signs are positive—sometimes they are a foretelling of future problems. But recognizing these signs is easier said than done, since not all are easily recognizable. They may be mistaken for mere coincidence, or they may be ignored completely. Here is what happened when Terry ignored his signs…

The day before leaving for a short work trip, Terry got an email from a friend saying that their pipes had burst. This friend lived north of Terry. He emailed back his sympathies but joked that that's what they got for moving to New Hampshire. He also told his friend that his family was welcome to stay at Terry's place in Connecticut while he was away. Terry's friend thanked him and said they were already getting the pipes fixed and everything should be good to go the following day.

Later that day, Terry went out for lunch with a couple of friends. They were enjoying their meals and a few drinks when they heard a commotion coming from the kitchen. A few minutes later, their waitress came over with the check.

"We're not done yet! We wanted another round," Terry's friends told the server.

"Oh, I'm terribly sorry. We have to ask you to finish up your meals and your drinks. I apologize again, but something has come up, so we have to close the restaurant," she responded.

"Is everyone okay?" Terry asked.

"Yes, and again, I apologize," she said.

"Well, that was strange," Terry said to the group after their server left the table. "I wonder what's going on?"

They finished their food and paid cash, leaving a good tip because although they could tell the server hadn't been happy about closing, she'd been very nice to them. As they were walking out, they heard a couple of the other workers talking about burst pipes in the kitchen. "Well that's too bad. I hope it doesn't close them down for too long," Terry said to his friends. Then the group said their goodbyes and promised to get together again soon.

Terry went back to his house and finished packing for his upcoming trip. He turned on the weather channel for some background noise. The weatherman was talking about a cold front moving through New York. Terry didn't pay much attention; he was leaving from Connecticut's Bradley International Airport early the next morning. He barely registered the weatherman saying that temperatures would continue to drop.

Terry got ready for bed and woke early the next day, making sure to turn the heat all the way down before he left so that he could save on his electric bill. On his way to the airport, he hit a bit of traffic. After a while, he got to the reason for the delay: a pipe had ruptured under the road, so they had to close two lanes of the highway. When Terry finally made it to the airport, he thought about how lucky he was to have gotten there in time to catch his plane.

The work trip was successful, and Terry returned to Connecticut a few days later. He was happy to be back after a few nights at a hotel; he'd had problems with the water there and couldn't wait to get home and take a real shower.

When Terry turned onto his street, he saw a bunch of city vehicles lining the road. He wondered what was going on, but he didn't stop to find out—he headed straight for home. Terry knew from the second he opened the door that something was wrong; he could just feel it. Still, he went upstairs and turned on the shower. But no water came out—there was just a hissing sound.

It turned out that cold front had made its way through Connecticut, and the pipes in Terry's house had burst. He'd turned the heat down too low and the pipes had frozen overnight. When he went downstairs, he discovered water leaking everywhere.

Looking back, Terry shared that all of the signs were there: "I was worried about trying to save a dollar or two and didn't think of the consequences. I wasn't paying attention at all." Had he only perceived what his intuition was trying to warn him about, he could have saved his pipes and his belongings, but more importantly, he wouldn't have had to redo so much of his home. Terry is convinced these signs were messages, and he totally ignored them.

Signs are not random messages that pop up for no reason. Generally, they are manifestations of your intuition attempting to tell you something. Sometimes a sign seeks you out, but you can also ask for a sign; next time you are struggling to make a decision, request a sign or two from the universe.

Granddaughter Crow

Many people ask for a sign—any sign—when they need guidance in whatever situation they are facing. We may request a sign that we are on the right path or doing the right thing. But one of the lesser-known ways to access universal guidance is to ask for a specific sign.

Instead of asking for a random sign, make the message more personalized. For example, if you want validation about a choice you're planning to make, you could ask to hear a horn blast or for a cardinal to fly across your path. Perhaps you ask to see a specific flower that is out of season. I recommend intuitively deciding on a symbol. This may add another layer to the importance of the sign and its meaning.

Granddaughter Crow does just this. She is the award-winning author of *Wisdom of the Natural World* and a healer who utilizes the messages she receives intuitively. She believes asking for a specific sign makes the experience feel less random and more intentional. In this way, she was able to find a job many years ago:

> I was in between jobs, meaning that I could see my income depleting and my expenses increasing. This is a time of scarcity, and some fear set in. So, I made an agreement with the universe (which is how the divine reveals itself to me). I simply focused—with my heart and future in my hands—and said, "I will follow the number thirty-three! This is what I will do. If you can hear me, please respond with the number thirty-three to lead me."
>
> I began to look for a job. Any job description that had the number thirty-three within it, I applied to. I found a company whose address had a thirty-three in it. I applied, interviewed, and got the job. My salary also had the number thirty-three in it. The number thirty-three led me to a job

that sustained me during a very difficult time. It was the perfect job at the perfect time.

I have found that the universe is always communicating with us. Sometimes we simply need to set up a code word, number, or symbol so that it can speak with us directly.

—Granddaughter Crow

By now, it should be clear that you can ask the universe for specific signs. However, always remain open to other signs that may show up, even if they aren't the specific sign you asked for. You don't want to limit yourself by waiting for just that one sign—you may miss other signs that are there! When you stay open-minded to the universe's messages, you have doubled the chance of receiving signs that can point you down your soul's path.

Deana

Deana, now a college professor and shamanic practitioner, was a big believer in all things metaphysical. After almost losing her legs—not to mention her life—in a horrific car accident, she went from working in an office as a graphic designer to learning about holistic practices, including the use of signs. Over time, Deana learned to trust that her angels were around to help her and regularly put them to work, asking for their help in many areas of her life. On one occasion, she asked for signs to confirm she'd found the house that was right for her and her husband.

Deana and her husband, Ralph, were house hunting. They were looking for their first home together, but nothing was jumping out at them. Because they were looking in three different towns, they had expected to find something easily, but when things weren't falling into place, they figured they'd take a break.

Even though they were taking a break from house hunting, Deana didn't want to totally give up. She decided to write to her angels to help her manifest the perfect home. She wrote what she wanted her dream house to be like and also stated that she wanted to receive three recognizable signs when she'd found the right place. She didn't specify what these signs would be, but left them open to the universe.

When Deana and Ralph decided to get back into house hunting, she was disappointed that she wasn't finding any houses that had even one sign or intuitive connection. One day, Deana and Ralph were out on a drive when she felt a nudge to take a left onto a residential street. It was a clairsentient feeling, something she was familiar with, so she went with it. After all, the two of them were just exploring, with nowhere in particular they had to be; they had nothing to lose by following Deana's nudge. As they drove down the street, they saw a bunch of wonderful houses, but none stuck out— and more importantly, there were no "For Sale" signs anywhere.

Then, they drove past a beautiful house with a sign out front. They hadn't seen it for sale online and quickly discovered why: it was a "For Sale by Owner" sign. Deana, determined not to ignore her intuition, was sure she had felt the nudge to turn onto this road for a reason. She wrote down the number on the sign and resolved to give the owner a call, even though she was sure the house would be way above their budget.

Later that day, Deana made the call. She was right: it was entirely too big of a house for them, not to mention way too expensive. However, Deana was pleased to discover that the woman who owned the property was very nice.

"Oh, I'm sorry it won't work out. Actually, we just got an offer that we are going to accept, so we couldn't have sold it to you anyway. But I promise if I hear of anything in the neighborhood, I will give you a call!" the owner said.

When Deana told Ralph, he said, "Oh well. We knew that would be a bust. It wasn't the right area."

Deana replied, "I actually think it is exactly what we need. Obviously not that house, but that area."

That night, Deana reiterated to her angels that she would wait for three signs. The next day, her cell phone buzzed. She recognized the number on the screen—it was the owner she had spoken to the day before! As she answered, she felt a bit shaky with excitement.

"Hi!" Deana exclaimed, a bit louder than she'd intended.

"Hi!" the woman answered cheerily. She then told Deana that one of her neighbors had decided to put their house on the market "For Sale by Owner" after seeing how quickly the woman's house had sold. She gave Deana the address and said the owners were expecting them. Deana and Ralph headed right over. As they drove, Deana found herself wondering if this house would show her the three signs she had asked for.

Before they'd even pulled into the driveway, Deana saw her first sign: the name of the road the house was on. It was the last name of Ralph's best friend, who had recently passed away. She took a mental note but didn't say anything about it.

As they pulled up to the house, Deana saw it was the right kind of house—the style, the size of property they were looking for, and the appropriate square footage—all things she had specified on her list of the perfect home. She couldn't wait to see the rest of the house.

The owners, a husband and wife, welcomed Deana and Ralph inside and gave them a tour. As they walked around the house, Deana saw another sign: the color hunter green was everywhere— her favorite color. Not only that, but the house had everything on her list.

The final sign came when Deana was chatting with the husband. It immediately felt like the two were old friends, and as they talked, they discovered they had something bizarre in common: both had been in bad car accidents in the past, leaving them with a permanent rod in their femur. Deana had never met or even heard of anyone else who shared this experience. That was the moment that clinched the deal. The house had everything on Deana's list, and the three signs were undeniable. It was like magic. This home was meant for Deana and Ralph, and they signed the paperwork a month later.

What are the odds? A skeptic could argue that the physical qualities of the house, the lot size, and even the predominance of the color hunter green were coincidences. But the street name being the last name of a recently deceased best friend? And the owner also having a rod in their femur? Those were much more than coincidences. Deana knew her angels had sent her the signs she needed to finalize the deal.

EXERCISE Asking for Specific Signs

Think about something you need guidance for, something that a yes or no answer would apply to. Then, decide on a sign you'd like receive for a "yes" answer and also a sign that represents a "no" answer.

Don't make it as simple as "If I see a blue car before a red one, that means yes," etc., because you will definitely see one or the other. Rather, ask for a sign that is not guaranteed. It may be cliché, but I like to use coins as signs; if I randomly see a coin on the ground heads up, that represents yes, whereas tails up means no.

Once you've decided what your question is and what your signs will be, it's time to be patient. You may have to give it a few days for your sign to show up, but don't be discouraged. It will happen when the time is right.

Synchronicities

Synchronicities are similar to signs in that they are external messages put in our paths so we notice them. They are like coincidences, but they are intentional, so they will keep showing up in our lives. When a synchronicity first occurs, we might not think much of it, but then we will notice it happening again and again and recognize it as a synchronistic event. Eventually, a synchronicity will reveal itself not as just one event, but as a combination of events that makes you say *Aha!* At times, it's difficult to recognize them, especially in the beginning. Because the first synchronistic event may be something random, we have to wait until we experience the next event to connect the dots and cement the synchronicities.

Alison DeNicola

One of my synchronistic events happened when I met Alison at a large new age conference in Colorado. Immediately, I felt drawn to her, and we became friends. Initially, I had no idea what she did, but I soon learned she is a prolific author and designer who works in the holistic field. She has won multiple awards for her card decks, including *Auspicious Symbols for Luck and Healing*. Alison has had plenty of experience with synchronicities:

> The path of tarot was a path of opening for my intuition. The first class I took opened my eyes to the art of interpretation. I continued to study, explore, and read for myself and others to gain insight, but more importantly, to work on my perception, intuitive development, and spiritual growth. My teacher offered weekly meditation circles with a focused intention on connecting with higher guidance and sharing the very basics of energy work, spiritual protection, and spiritual hygiene.

This was my elementary education, and it was helping to support the unseen growth that was happening quite rapidly with my intuition.

Several years after those first tarot classes and many tarot readings for friends and strangers, I began looking for a part-time job. I scanned the local classified ads, searching for part-time work that would fit into the school day and provide me with an outlet for my energy. Intuitively, I was drawn to an ad, and after some quick emails back and forth, I had an interview lined up with a well-known company that published tarot decks.

I've now been associated with the company for many years, and I believe this to be a result of developing and following my intuition. Many amazing things have happened as a result of that early "nudge"; I have written eight oracle decks, taught many spiritual-based classes, and led people on international retreats. In reflection, all of this is a beautiful result of trusting my inner voice and following inner guidance.

—Alison DeNicola

Though you may not always recognize synchronistic events as they're unfolding, following your instincts will prove fortuitous more often than not, and when you look back on your journey, it will all make sense.

Sandra

Sandra had a synchronistic experience that she didn't understand until the very end. When it all clicked, she was ecstatic! Two weeks before she understood what was going on, she was driving to work. On the way, she noticed a beautiful Mustang convertible. It was bright blue, an extraordinary color, and one that stood out. Sandra thought the car was really cool, but in no time her train of thought had wandered to something else.

That day, Sandra went out for lunch with a coworker. When they got to the restaurant, they chose to sit outside on the patio. The two were chatting about nothing in particular when her coworker interrupted their conversation by saying, "Wow, that's a nice car!"

Sandra looked up to see the car she was talking about: a Mustang convertible. It was bright green, an unusual color for a car; it certainly was attention-grabbing. She responded, "That sure is cool—I'm a little jealous!" and then resumed their conversation.

On her way home from work, Sandra noticed *another* Mustang. This one wasn't a convertible, but it was a bright yellow that really stood out. She loved it. As she drove home in her practical Volvo, she daydreamed about what it would be like to drive a Mustang on the highway, shifting gears, hair flying. It was a nice fantasy—one she quickly forgot about as she got home, hung out with her family, and went to bed.

The next day, Sandra woke up to her kids jumping on her. She'd almost forgotten it was her forty-second birthday! Her kids told her to hurry up and get dressed because they had made her breakfast. When her kids made breakfast, it usually consisted of semi-burnt toast and runny scrambled eggs, which was fine by Sandra; she knew they did it because they loved her.

She made her way to the kitchen, where her food was waiting with a single bright yellow flower. Sandra sat down and drank a sip of the orange juice they'd poured for her. Then she noticed there weren't any other plates on the table.

"Aren't you eating?" she asked her family.

Her husband and children smiled back, looking like Cheshire cats. The kids giggled a little and she knew something was up, but she shrugged and started eating breakfast. Then, she bit into something hard. When she took the object out of her mouth, she recognized it as one of those car pieces from the game of Monopoly.

"What is this? Do you guys want to play Monopoly?" Sandra asked.

"No, Mom! Close your eyes. Wait, put on your shoes first!" her kids shouted.

Sandra looked at her husband, who still had that Cheshire cat grin on his face.

"Come on, honey. It's nothing bad, I promise," he said.

Sandra let her husband cover her eyes as the kids walked her outside. They yelled, "One, two, three, open your eyes! Surprise!"

In front of her was a yellow Mustang convertible with a bright red bow on the hood.

Sandra realized the Mustangs she had noticed the day before were her intuition talking. Initially, she hadn't put it together as an intuitive message, although she now understood the synchronicity. Thank goodness Sandra's intuition didn't spoil the surprise!

As you can see, there are plenty of happy synchronistic stories. I love it when synchronicities have a happy ending, especially if you're not expecting it. When that last piece clicks into place, it can leave you awestruck. However, that doesn't mean that seeing a cool car a few times is a synchronistic sign that someone is going to gift you one. (I have to remind my husband of this all the time.)

Remember that synchronicities can be small events too—they are not always going to be grand gestures or life-changing events. Of course it's fantastic when that happens, but celebrate the little things too. What do small synchronicities look like? Let's say you see a specific kind of coffee at the grocery store and think, *Hmm, that looks good*, but you walk by it and continue shopping. Then you go down a totally different aisle, and there on the endcap is a display of that same coffee. You think, *Hmm, what a coincidence*, but you don't put the coffee in your cart. When you go to check out after you're done shopping, you see that someone left a container of that same coffee in the bagging area by accident. *Hmm!* That is a synchronicity.

Now, with that being said, I want to emphasize that marketers are professionals when it comes to getting a customer to buy their product. If you keep seeing an ad for something, that's probably all it is. But if there's a kicker—let's say that when you get home, your spouse asks if you got his text requesting that specific brand of coffee—that's a sign you've been ignoring the synchronicities. And trust me, this sort of thing happens! The key is to be aware. Continue to allow your awareness to expand so that you can recognize those nudges as signs and not just great marketing.

EXERCISE Recognizing Synchronicity

Recognizing synchronicities can be difficult because you have to wait for a second, third, or fourth thing to happen before you notice the pattern. You won't even realize you're waiting!

To strengthen your ability to recognize synchronicities, carry a journal with you. As you go about your day, write down anything that makes you question what just happened, as well as anything that makes you say "Aha!" If, later on, you experience another synchronistic event that coordinates with your initial discovery, write that down too. You will get better at deciphering these occurrences the more you practice.

Sometimes We Ask for Them, Sometimes They Are Just There

Sometimes signs and synchronicities are in your face and there's no denying them. However, it's just as likely that we will take them for granted; we don't always recognize them for what they are. Signs and synchronicities are like all intuitive gifts: the more we acknowledge their reality, the more we can identify them. The same is true of denying their existence, which will make it harder to identify signs and synchronicities. It may take a bit of time to truly recognize, credit, and value your intuition.

PRO TIP

The more open you are to signs and synchronicities, the more often they will show up to help you.

Chapter 8

DREAMS AND HELPERS FROM THE OTHER SIDE

Have you ever woken up and wondered what just happened? Dreaming is a nightly occurrence for a lot of people, but sometimes we have dreams that make us question whether what we dreamt about actually happened. When we wake up scratching our heads, it's often a clue that we should explore the meaning of a dream further.

People dream for a variety of reasons. One of the reasons is to process events, typically events that our conscious or subconscious mind can't or doesn't want to process while awake. Another explanation is that when we dream, we review memories of things we've done. The cause of our dream may simply be what we ingested before bed: food, drink, drugs, etc. One more reason we dream—the reason we are interested in for the purposes of this book—is that this is yet another way our intuition talks to us.

Intuitive Dreams

Dreams sometimes let you know you've been ignoring your intuition by sharing the messages you missed during your waking state. You can even have precognitive dreams of what's to come. Dreams can also be your intuition, or your soul, sharing a lesson. Perhaps your intuition is alerting you to a certain topic in your life that you should investigate, one that you may not recognize in your waking moments; think of these as teaching dreams or dreams that are trying to connect the unconscious to your conscious self. And, as you'll see later in this chapter, dreams can also be visitations from a loved one or even one of your guides.

Mat Auryn

Mat Auryn has been drawn to the metaphysical world since he was a child. He is a witch and sought-after speaker who has helped thousands of people with his psychic abilities and tarot readings. His best-selling books on the occult have won multiple awards and include *Mastering Magick* and *Psychic Witch*. However, all of that may not have happened had he not had a prophetic dream that changed the trajectory of his life:

> I had recently moved to the East Coast, and despite having an almost impeccable work history and fantastic references, I couldn't find a job. I began looking for one everywhere and eventually got a full-time job working at a bagel shop for minimum wage. Then, on a trip to Salem, I saw a sign that a store was looking for tarot readers.
>
> Trusting my gut, I asked the person behind the counter about it. The owner was in earshot and asked if I would be willing to give him a reading as an interview. He hired me on

the spot and asked me to come in on Monday to start part-time. I was thrilled! Not only did I find another job temporarily, but I would be doing something that I loved.

But I had to make a decision. As a Pisces, I tend to want to take a nap when I feel overwhelmed emotionally, so I decided to take a nap before I chose between a stable job that I hated and an unstable part-time job based on commission and tips, but one that I had always dreamed of doing professionally. As I drifted to sleep, I felt pretty devastated because I figured I would need to turn down the tarot gig in Salem and return to the job I hated that paid the bills.

Then I woke from a dream where a goddess came to me and told me that I was at a crossroads and that this choice would significantly impact my whole life path. She asked me if I truly trusted her or not.

I decided to do a tarot reading for myself about the situation. Despite defying logic, the reading said I should choose the path of spirituality, or I'd lose everything. I double-checked and triple-checked and kept getting the same messages, and I felt it deeply in my gut that the cards were right. So, like the Fool card in the tarot, I decided to take a leap of faith and texted my boss at the bagel shop, apologized, and said I had found another job and wouldn't return to bagel life.

Over time, I became a pretty popular tarot reader at the shop, and since customers were asking to get readings from me, I was getting scheduled more regularly. This transition allowed me to begin putting together workshops to teach, many of which would later evolve into my book *Psychic Witch*. My new work also allowed me the time to write. The book ended up being much more successful than I ever could have predicted, and needless to say, I'm not living in a tiny trailer on the East Coast anymore and have devoted my whole life to the spiritual path of teaching and writing.

So, what about the cards warning that I would lose everything if I didn't trust the leap of faith? A week into working as a tarot reader, I ran into an old coworker. The bagel shop had shut down. Everyone had lost their jobs there permanently. If I had chosen the logical choice out of fear of security and not trusted all the signs, I would be back at square one searching for a job, and my life wouldn't be what it is today.

—Mat Auryn

Mat followed his dream, literally. Even though he was afraid of his choice, it was the perfect one for him. He's been intuitive his entire life, and it has led him to be extremely successful—who knows what would have happened if he hadn't taken the job as a tarot reader!

Ann

Ann, now a retired nurse, can vividly remember a dream she had when she was a kid, way back in the 1940s. A family friend, Julie, had just announced that she was going to work on a cruise ship as a server and, as she put it, see the world. She was very excited, and everyone was thrilled for her. Back then, there weren't too many cruise ships out there, and even less opportunity to work on one; everyone thought Julie was extremely lucky. They were setting out for the far north on Julie's first trip. The trip was scheduled to take at least a few weeks, though they weren't sure exactly how long it would take, so Julie had packed for a month.

A few days after Julie left on her voyage, Ann had a dream. In the dream, she saw a newspaper headline about a cruise ship sinking. All aboard had perished. The newspaper spun in a circle, and it actually made her dizzy. When Ann woke up, she told her mother about the dream.

"It looked so real. I'm scared for Julie and everyone else on the boat!" Ann exclaimed.

"It will be fine. There's nothing to worry about—you're thinking of the Titanic. You are probably just missing Julie," Ann's mom said.

Julie wasn't aboard the Titanic, which had sunk decades earlier; she was on a smaller, lesser-known ship. But even with her mother's reassurance, Ann couldn't get the image of the newspaper headline out of her mind. She had a bad feeling in her stomach.

An hour or so after she told her mom about the dream, the paper boy delivered the newspaper. Ann was about to run outside to get it, but her mom told her to calm down and finish getting ready for school. She'd taken too long to eat and chat about her dream—she'd be late if she didn't hurry.

So, Ann went to school, but she fretted the entire day. She couldn't shake the bad feeling in her stomach. After school, she practically ran all the way home, and as soon as she stepped into the house, she shouted, "Mom! Where are you?"

Her mother walked into the room, wiping her hands on her apron. She told Ann to sit down.

Once they were seated, she said, "There's some bad news, Ann." She held out the newspaper. Sure enough, the headline on the front revealed that Julie's cruise ship had gone down and there were no known survivors. The two of them cried for a bit. Eventually, Ann sat down to do her homework and her mom made dinner. That night, before bed, Ann stated that she never wanted to receive information like that again.

That was the only time Ann had a prophetic dream. When she looks back on it now, she wonders if the dream was trying to help her prepare for Julie's death. Some may question why Ann requested not to have any other intuitive dreams. She didn't want to see any other bad news in her dreams—it scared her too much to be right.

Marley

Mercifully, not all dreams are foretellers of doom and gloom. Many dreams have positive messages. Marley shared her dream with me, and unlike Ann's story, Marley's melted my heart!

Marley had just finished college, and she was debating breaking up with her boyfriend. They'd been together a little under a year, and the longer they were together, the more she disliked the relationship. But here's the rub: like many people, Marley was worried about trading her not-so-great relationship for no relationship at all.

For about a month, she reflected on her relationship, and what kept coming up was that she wasn't happy, but she was afraid she wouldn't find someone better. After all, she thought maybe she was just being too picky. On paper, he was a great catch. He'd just graduated college and already had a job at a big investment firm. Marley had also just graduated but was having a hard time finding work as a pharmacist near where she lived; eventually, she accepted a job as a pharmacy technician. She figured a breakup adding stress to her life would only make her less happy, so she stayed with him.

Before falling asleep, Marley started asking to dream about what she should do. For weeks, she didn't get any helpful messages while she was sleeping. This had a negative effect on her, as she would wake up in the morning disappointed. So, finally, she stopped asking. That seemed to be the essential twist for Marley, because that night she *did* dream.

In her dream, Marley saw a man with reddish-brown hair, down on one knee in front of her. He was cute and his eyes were warm and friendly. He had laugh lines on his young face, which she loved.

When she woke up the next morning, a single teardrop rolled down her cheek. She wanted to keep dreaming! But she doubted that this dream had a deeper meaning; if it did, wouldn't she have been shown more?

Still, when Marley was with her boyfriend that night, she kept seeing the dream man in her mind. She couldn't get him out of her thoughts. Meanwhile, everything her boyfriend did that evening annoyed her. They were at a local seafood restaurant that he liked, but Marley didn't care much for it: she didn't eat seafood. This was typical and one of the things that drove her crazy. Her boyfriend always did things like this; he'd want to go to dinner at "You know, that place we love!" But in reality, *he* was the one who always loved the places they went and the things they did. It hit her like a ton of bricks as the date wrapped up—she was done.

As she came to this realization, Marley saw a flash of her dream man, and it gave her the strength she needed to tell her boyfriend she didn't want to do it anymore; she was done with their relationship. He answered, "Oh, okay. So, do you want to pay for half of this?"

After almost a year, this was the kind of answer she should have expected. Although she still felt a bit insecure about being alone, Marley knew that this was definitely the right thing to do. This was confirmed for her when she ran into her ex-boyfriend two days later and he had his arm wrapped around a new girl. Marley repeatedly told herself she was going to be okay as she walked into work the next morning. It's not like they lived together or anything; she (hopefully) would never have to see him again.

The pharmacist Marley worked with was a nice older lady with grown children. They had a good rapport and Marley was looking forward to her advice. As her shift began, she filled in her coworker on her dream, the breakup, and running into her ex.

"Well, honey, you'll be okay. In fact, you'll be better than okay. He doesn't deserve you, and you will find someone who does. Although, that will be really hard, because you're a great catch!" she responded.

After the pharmacist finished her sentence, Marley turned toward the front desk, smiling. And there he was. Her dream man was standing right in front of her!

The man smiled at Marley and said, "I agree—I bet you're a great catch."

They both blushed. She couldn't believe it was him! After Marley showed him where to find the ibuprofen he needed, they struck up a conversation and even exchanged numbers. The whole time, the pharmacist just stared at them with her jaw dropped. When her dream man wasn't looking, Marley turned and mouthed to her, "It's him!" He was there, in the flesh, and better than she could have possibly imagined.

They went out that night and married a year later. They are still together, and the two of them are building a happy family: they have a one-year-old and a new baby on the way! If Marley hadn't valued her dream, she may have forgotten it in the morning, or she may have discounted it when she saw the man as just a premonition of an upcoming workday. But Marley believed in the intuitive message in her dream; it gave her the strength to break up with her ex, and it led her to her now husband!

EXERCISE Asking for Answers

Intuition can randomly talk to us through our dreams, but we can also request for an answer to come through in our dreams. Granddaughter Crow, a natural healer quoted in chapter 7, shared, "Sometimes we make it harder than it has to be, and we make our intuition work harder to communicate with us. I suggest that we simply relax and fall asleep. Our intuition will always come through, and it tends to come through when we are more relaxed and let go of the outcome. Dreams are a wonderful way that our intuition speaks with us!"

Tonight, right before you go to sleep, ask for an answer to a specific question you may have. The question could be about anything: which direction to take, whether or not to pursue a new job, etc. Then, place a journal and a pen beside your bed before you fall asleep.

As soon as you wake, write down everything you remember from your dreams. Was there anything specific? If so, describe it in detail so you can refer back to your notes. Also, if your dreams had any directions, you may need to follow them—they will be easier to remember if you take the time to write them down.

Did your question get answered? If so, great! If not, ask again the next night, or ask a different question you may have. Then, on the third night, don't ask for anything. Notice if you dream more or less either way.

Denise

Some dreams are fantastic premonitions of things to come. Others, though, are warnings.

Denise, a realtor, had bought her twin boys used cars prior to them getting their driver's licenses. They were both so excited and couldn't wait to drive them. When they got their licenses, her sons immediately drove their cars to meet up with friends. They loved the freedom owning a vehicle gave them.

A couple days later, Denise was shaken up when she woke. She'd had a dream that her boys had gone for a drive with a friend in one of their cars. In her dream, the car hit a tree, and one of her sons died. Denise couldn't get this vision out of her head. She felt like the dream was a portent of bad things to come.

That day, Denise decided that she had to sell the cars. The boys complained, but not after she said she would buy them newer, safer cars. They all got in her minivan and went car shopping that same day. Both cars were traded in for two SUVs, which were stronger and sturdier. Denise was happy and, surprisingly, the boys were cool with having bigger cars too. They liked being higher up.

A month went by without incident. Denise's sons were loving their new vehicles and took turns driving to and from school. They realized, after a week or so, that driving both cars used twice the amount of gas; considering they did the same after-school activities, they agreed it was better to drive together. Not to mention the fact that her boys liked having each other to talk to on their commute to school. They had the same agreement when going out with their friends at night: because they shared so many of the same friends, it just made sense to drive together.

About a month after they'd gotten their licenses, the boys and one of their friends went for a ride. Denise had a weird feeling all night and confided in her husband. They finally got into bed, but neither was able to sleep. Later, while they were still lying in bed, the cops called. An officer told them the kids had been in an accident but didn't tell them much more than the location where the accident had occurred. Denise and her husband leapt into their vehicle and headed over.

On the way there, Denise's husband said, "It's okay, honey. If someone had died, they would have warned us!" He was trying to convince himself as much as her.

When they got to the accident, the scene was horrific. The SUV was wrapped around a tree. Denise turned as white as a ghost, and she had to grab on to her husband's arm so she didn't fall down. He had to maneuver to hold her up.

"It's the tree from the dream! Oh my God!" she cried.

As if on cue, the boys came out from behind the police cruiser, wrapped in blankets but barely scratched. Denise and her husband could not hold back their joy seeing them. The boys were a bit shaken up but otherwise fine.

"Mom, it's a good thing you got us those SUVs instead. The cop said if we had been in any other car, at least one of us would have been killed," one of the boys said.

Denise told her kids that from then on, they needed to run their possible car purchases by her and her intuition first, even when they were old!

Jenna Matlin

Jenna Matlin is a professional psychic and the author of *Will You Give Me a Reading?* From an early age, Jenna knew she was gifted. Occasionally, her dreams warned her of things to come, so she learned to take them seriously. She knows that every dream that feels like an intuitive nudge is one, and she pays attention to those messages. As we've discussed, prophetic dreams don't have to be about ourselves. In fact, quite often, Jenna's involve other people:

A couple of years ago, I dreamt that my mother-in-law was in the hospital, and she was dying. I woke up and turned to my husband and told him. I hesitated to tell him, as I did not want to upset him, but I am really glad that I did.

He called his mother that morning and everything appeared fine, so we let it go. Two days later, we got a call from my sister-in-law. She told us my mother-in-law had been in the hospital overnight due to an issue with her kidneys, but they let her go with a prescription.

Despite being told by the doctor that she did not have much of a problem, my husband implored his mom to go back to the emergency room. My dream showed me that the situation was probably worse than what was first thought, and it was. Turns out, my mother-in-law had a kidney infection that was on the cusp of going septic, and she needed a hospital stay that included intravenous antibiotics for a couple of days.

I am very relieved and glad that my dream was prophetic enough to give us the information we needed to take a course of action that resulted in her being around longer, as I like my mother-in-law!

—Jenna Matlin

Dreams and Helpers from the Other Side

Clients often ask me about their dreams. I share with them that what they are experiencing is not always just a dream—it's quite possibly a visitation. What does this mean for them, or for you? It means that your helpers may be coming through to share wisdom they have, or to simply say hello and let you know they see what's going on in your life. Like premonitory dreams, they may provide information about things to be on the lookout for or things to come. This often happens during your dream state because your conscious mind isn't in the way.

Each one of us has a whole bunch of helpers. Our guides, of which we have many, are often mistaken for angels or guardian angels. On occasion, angels do show up. But, in my professional experience, it's most often guides and deceased loved ones who get mistaken for guardian angels. However, angels will show up to help us in life-and-death situations. You may also be visited by an archangel, like Michael; Michael is a powerful archangel who helps fight against evil and helps you keep the faith. Raphael, another archangel, is a healer who may show up when we need major healing. Angels have no direct connection to deceased loved ones or even guides. They've never walked the earth and are ethereal helpers.

The most frequent helpers we encounter are our deceased loved ones. These are people who were either part of our family or close friends who died. Frequently, we are visited by loved ones from many generations ago; they haven't walked the earth in a while. Interestingly enough, our guides are often people that lived many years ago who have gone through multiple lifetimes and acquired a vast amount of knowledge. It's not critical to always know who is showing up to help you, but at times they'll let you know who they are, and you'll know why they're there.

Maria

Maria, a creative arts teacher, woke up feeling confused for a variety of reasons. She'd had a really strange dream, though upon waking, she understood that it was a visitation from her Aunt Netta. She'd always believed in intuition but hadn't dreamt of her aunt before. It felt like she'd really talked to Netta in her dream, but it got kind of weird. A family, the Morans, showed up in her dream. She recognized this family and knew they were all still alive, so she didn't know what to make of this—even in her dream she was kind of bewildered. Maria hadn't seen this particular family in a long time, so she didn't understand why they were there. The Morans were all sitting at a rectangular table in what Maria described as a European plaza or piazza, somewhere she'd never been in real life. The whole area was surrounded by big, ornate buildings.

Maria dreamt that she walked up to the family and said, "Hi, this is Maria!" She thought that was strange because they all knew her. She wondered why she would have said that and in that way. She also felt strange because the dream was in black and white, which was unusual for her; she tended to dream in color. (Side note: this is uncommon—it's usually the other way around.) Even in her dream, Maria was questioning why things were happening the way they were.

The next thing she knew, Maria was talking with her aunt, who was surrounded by a bright, blinding light.

"Aunt Netta! What's it like there?!?!" Maria shouted. She could feel herself slowly coming out of her dream.

Netta floated away in the light, saying, "It's beautiful, Maria."

"No! Don't go! Stay! I have more questions!" Maria shrieked desperately, to no avail. She woke up, and her aunt was gone.

Now fully awake and even more puzzled, Maria couldn't figure out what the dream had been about or whether it had a message for her. But she knew her aunt was coming to her from the other side; it had definitely been a visitation. She puzzled over the dream for a day or two, then let it go.

Three weeks later, Maria unexpectedly ran into one of the members of the Moran family at the grocery store. This particular store was a place Maria didn't usually frequent. The fact that she was there shopping and then ran into one of the people from her dream struck her as an uncanny coincidence—and she didn't believe in coincidences. So, she stopped Mr. Moran.

"Oh, wow—I had a dream about you guys. Is everybody okay? I dreamt your family was hanging out in, like, Italy with my Aunt Netta."

Mr. Moran was a family friend, so Maria knew he would understand the reference. He responded, "Everybody's great. Maybe your aunt just missed us?"

They laughed and talked for a few more minutes. He promised to tell everyone she said hello, and as they were walking away, she turned and said, "Make sure you all take care of yourselves."

A week later, she found out that Mr. Moran was in the hospital. If Maria hadn't run into him at the grocery store, he may not have thought anything of the pain he had in his chest. He could have waited too long to go to the hospital. Luckily, he remembered Maria's dream and got the pain checked out. Maria is convinced her Aunt Netta showed up in her dream to help her help the Moran family. Her aunt's presence alerted her that it was important to pay attention to the dream.

Hope

One night, Hope dreamt of her family's lake house. Before Hope's mom died, she had intentionally purchased a lake house in Connecticut, between Massachusetts and New Jersey, where her two daughters lived. She wanted a place the family could come together and celebrate that was halfway for her daughters' families, so the lake house was in an ideal location.

Hope had dreamt of the lake house before, so this was not unusual. What was strange was who was in her dream, and where they were sitting. Hope, her deceased mother, her father, and his new girlfriend, Danielle, were all sitting in the hot tub together, with Hope's father sitting next to her mother. Hope was surprised to see Danielle in her dream, as she was not crazy about the new woman and was having a hard time allowing her to be part of their lives.

In her dream, Hope's mother turned to her and said, "Tell your dad to go sit next to Danielle and put his arm around her." When Hope looked toward her father, she saw that he was now sitting with his arm around Danielle, almost hesitantly, but he was smiling.

Hope woke suddenly and felt one single tear roll down her face. She knew that her mom had visited her to let her know it was okay for her father to date someone new, and that it was okay to welcome a new romantic interest into the family home. Hope believes her mom also wanted to let her know that she'd always be around.

Zack

Zack had a dream that someone he knew was very sick, but it wasn't clear who. Sadness washed over him. Oddly enough, in the dream, he also felt that he was going to get really good news soon. When Zack woke up, he couldn't quite figure out how the good news was connected to the sadness. None of it made sense—everyone he knew was fine.

Then, his phone rang. It turned out his mother was, indeed, sick. She was at the hospital because she'd had what doctors believed to be a heart attack. Her doctor told Zack they didn't know if his mother was going to make it through the week. As the news settled in, Zack understood why he'd felt so sad in his dream.

But, just like in his dream, Zack got some good news shortly after. Contrary to the doctor's warning, his mother's tests came back better than they'd hoped, and she was expected to make a full recovery. Zack now understood the ending of his dream and was extremely happy about it.

Hello? Wakey, Wakey!

Before you discount your dreams, think about whether they may have been visitations or, quite possibly, your intuition conveying some information. Our dreams often play an important role in the comprehension of things we are too busy to understand when we are awake. If you are lucky enough to have a loved one come through, consider it a bonus.

Helpers in the Waking World

We've lived, we've loved, and we've all known someone who passed away. These loved ones can show up in your dreams or while you're awake. Regardless of how they come to you, they always have a reason. It may be to tell you they love you and are still around, they may have an important message to deliver, or they may merely be nudging you in the right direction.

What's interesting is that so often our guides and loved ones send us information that we don't necessarily differentiate from our own intuition. Sometimes, yes, we do recognize they've come through and comprehend they are imparting some kind of wisdom. For example, we may experience this more externally; messages may sound like they are coming from outside of us rather than inside our minds, almost as though someone is talking to us. Other times, they help us better recognize and understand our own intuitive senses. But they don't always need to be acknowledged as the messengers. Rather, it's more important that we identify the intuitive impressions we get from all positive sources—ourselves *and* our helpers.

Again, your deceased loved ones and other helpers will come through any way they can. When it's crucial, you'll usually get more than one metaphysical nudge to make you pay attention to their guidance. They don't always bring vital messages; sometimes they're simply guiding you toward what will be good for you. Other times, it's just to let you know all is well.

Abby

Abby's good friend Katie was a health fanatic. Because of that, Abby felt incredulity and disbelief when Katie passed way too early. She was only twenty-five years old and never should have died the way she did: she had lung cancer—though she hadn't smoked a day in her life. It was sudden and it took her fast, leaving behind her husband and their five-year-old daughter. There wasn't a dry eye in the church on the day of the funeral.

Abby ended up sitting right behind Katie's family, which made her even sadder. She couldn't stop thinking about how Katie's daughter would have to grow up without her mom. As Abby sat there crying, she suddenly felt Katie's presence. She had a message for Abby. Katie said, "Do not be sad. When people die, it is like leaving a child at daycare. The child has no concept of time and does not know when they will see the parent again, but the parent knows—same as the deceased person."

Abby felt her friend's words in her soul. Katie had shown up at her own funeral to comfort her good friend in the best possible way. What she'd impressed upon Abby has stayed with her and helped her throughout her whole life.

Eva

Eva, a preschool teacher at a Jewish temple, experienced her mom coming through when she sold her late mother's house. When Eva's mom died, the whole family helped get her home ready for sale, and they listed it together. They were ready to say goodbye to it.

During the open house, a young couple came in. The couple shared that the property wasn't exactly what they were looking for, but they lived in the area and had seen the For Sale signs, so they decided to check it out. As Eva took the couple on a tour of the house, she noticed the woman admiring her late mother's quilts.

As they talked, the couple commented on the quilts that were displayed on the beds. The woman told Eva that she had just gotten into quilting herself and was really enjoying it. She loved the detail and the delicate stitching that Eva's mother's quilts showed. Actually, she told Eva, she was very impressed with one in particular; she brought Eva to the room it was in to show her.

Eva took the quilt off the bed. "Here. You need to have it."

"Oh no! I can't take your mother's quilt. Especially since we were just stopping in," the woman responded.

"Yes, actually, you can. I feel like my mom wants you to have it. It doesn't matter if you buy the house or not."

After many thanks, the couple left, holding the quilt made by Eva's mother. And then, lo and behold, the couple came back within the hour and put in an offer. They couldn't do more than asking price—in fact, they were going to be just below because they couldn't afford more than that—but they'd felt pulled back to the house and knew it had to be theirs.

Eva quickly discussed the offer with her family. Everyone agreed that Eva's mom had brought the couple to the house, but there was one problem: they had all wanted a young couple with small children to buy the house. After some more conversation, Eva learned that the couple did have a toddler, and there was another baby on the way. Eva and her family knew this was meant to be, and it was a done deal.

To this day, Eva believes her mom brought the couple to the house so they could enjoy it as her family had done for generations. When they closed on the house, Eva felt a sense of relief that she'd done the right thing and followed her mother's wishes—both when she was alive and after.

EXERCISE Connecting with Deceased Loved Ones and/or Guides

Have you ever felt your loved ones around you? Perhaps you felt their guidance or just a warm hug. This exercise can help you connect with deceased loved ones, or you can use it to discover your guides, or both!

Before you begin, make sure you are somewhere you can relax. Close your eyes and breathe deeply. Then imagine you are at a beach, sitting on perfectly warm sand. Look toward the water. Coming out of the waves, walking toward you, is a familiar face. Who is it? What is their name? Ask if they have a message for you.

Notice if there's anyone else coming out of the water and walking toward you. If so, ask if they have any messages for you.

Do the messages you've received make sense? Ask your visitors if there's anything else they want to share with you. You can even ask them a specific question you need help with. When you are done talking, thank them, then watch them float away on the water until they safely disappear.

If your visitor told you they love you or simply smiled without saying anything, that's common. Don't dismay! Accept the visit with gratitude.

When you're ready, wiggle your toes and fingers to ground yourself. Open your eyes and come back to your present space. If you'd like, write down everything you saw or heard so you can revisit what you discovered.

You can do this exercise any time you need to ask for help or feel disconnected from your spiritual support system. They are there for you!

Layla

Layla, a sixteen-year-old, was at the Department of Motor Vehicles, taking the written exam for her driver's permit. It was her second time around; the first time, she failed the test because she ignored her intuition on the last question. This time, she was second-guessing the final question. Layla was running out of time, but she couldn't make up her mind. If she got this last question wrong, she might fail for the second time.

She was getting herself all worked up. So, she closed her eyes and silently asked for help. Almost immediately, she felt guided to choose a different letter for the final multiple-choice question. Again, she doubted herself. Then, Layla felt a nudge, almost pushing her finger on the keyboard, and she felt Grammy there with her, helping her. She knew what she had to do.

Layla listened to her deceased grandmother and passed the exam. She was fortunate: when Layla doubted her intuitive message, her grandmother gave her a second nudge to make sure she knew it was real. She could feel her grandmother's energy and followed Grammy's guidance all the way to her brand new driver's permit.

Allie

It's not unusual for parents or grandparents to help their family from the other side. Occasionally, other people's parents will come through in some way, benefiting their family with your assistance. The deceased may use you as a messenger when it's the best way to make something happen.

Allie, a volunteer coordinator, was out shopping for clothes. She was mainly browsing because she did not have a lot of money. When Allie saw a purple top, she immediately felt drawn to it. It wasn't her style, and it was kind of expensive, so she didn't understand why she was feeling pulled to the shirt. Then, Allie felt a strong urge to buy the shirt for a woman she knew but was not good friends with.

In that moment, Allie was conflicted because she knew she didn't have the extra funds. The shirt was more than she'd normally spend on herself, let alone a woman she barely knew, but she felt like someone was telling her she couldn't pass it up. Allie strongly believed we get intuitive notions for a reason, so she bought the top. She had to buy it—there was no leaving the store without it.

After she left the store, Allie thought, *How am I going to give this shirt to that woman, as I don't really know her? This is going to seem kind of weird!* She decided to just be honest. So, Allie Facebook messaged the woman and told her that she had felt the urge to buy her a purple top. She sent a picture of the shirt along with the message.

The woman she'd bought the top for immediately messaged her back and told her she was crying happy tears. She went on to tell Allie that her dad had recently passed, and she had been feeling very down. Purple was her favorite color, and she really liked the brand of clothing the shirt was. Allie's message brought the woman so much joy.

When Allie told me this story, she said it had to have been the woman's dad who nudged her to buy the shirt. Otherwise, she never would have. The shirt ended up fitting the woman perfectly, and now Allie and her previously distant acquaintance have become friends, all thanks to the woman's dad—and Allie's intuition.

For those of us who've experienced intuitive nudges from spirit, we don't always know who is coming to our aid. It's possible that we did not even know the person when they were alive. But we'll usually recognize that the nudge is actually coming from someone, and we are generally able to figure out who, even if it's after the fact. Not being sure who is nudging you doesn't discount spirit's message. And don't worry, spirit doesn't mind if you can't identify them. As long as you acknowledge the intuitive nudge, they're happy. Plus, as Heather experienced, the spirit may not even be human.

Shari and Heather

Heather had been having a very hard time. She was just a kid, but she'd been in and out of the hospital many times due to an undiagnosed issue. After yet another hospital visit, Heather worried that the doctors may never figure out what was wrong. Heather's mom, Shari, was also very concerned about her daughter, though she told Heather she knew intuitively that Heather would be okay and live a long life. Even though she trusted her gut feeling, Shari was deeply worried. As a mother, there was no quelling her fears—until one day.

Heather went to her mom and told her she'd been lying in her bed, looking at a book, wondering when the next time she'd get admitted to the hospital would be. As Heather said this, Shari teared up a bit, not wanting her daughter to be scared or sad. But, with a smile, Heather told her it wasn't a bad thing.

"Mom, no, I'm not worried. Travy came to me. He told me he knew everything would be all right, and now I know that I'm going to be okay!" Heather exclaimed.

"Wow," Shari responded. "That is amazing! That makes me so happy!"

They both believed in intuition and trusted that Travy, a deceased loved one, really had shown up. Now, you may be wondering if Travy was Heather's uncle or grandpa. Nope! Travy was the family dog. Before he passed, Heather and Travy had snuggled and played together constantly. They were very close, so it made total sense their family pup was still with Heather.

About an hour later, Shari found herself worrying again. Although she believed in Travy's visit and it had made her a bit more hopeful, she was still concerned. Her mind could not rest; thoughts were churning in her head. So, Shari prayed. She prayed to all her helpers on the other side.

Then Shari looked up and saw her grandfather, Heather's great-grandfather. He was visiting from the other side. As Shari looked at him in awe, her grandfather essentially repeated what

Travy had said: Heather was going to survive this, and Shari was going to help her, even though she didn't know how yet.

This was very validating for Shari. Both Travy and Shari's grandfather had shown up—on the same day—to confirm that Heather was going to make it through this years-long ordeal. Sure enough, they were right. Shari paid closer attention to her intuition after these visitations, and she helped Heather get better. She changed their way of life; the two began eating healthy and exercising, and Shari wholeheartedly believes that this is what has kept her daughter out of the hospital since. Shari and Heather are fully aware of the importance of visitations from deceased loved ones—both human and animal.

Bill

Bill was a runner who ran every day. One day, he started getting incredible cramps in his legs during his run—so much so that he had to stop. He waited for a bit, rubbing his legs while he sat. It wasn't getting better, so he decided to walk home. On the way, he began thinking he really had to get to the doctor. His intuition was telling him it was more than just a cramp, and that it was important for him to have his leg cramps checked out.

When Bill got home, his mom came into the room. He lived with his parents, but his father had passed away recently, so it was currently just him and his mom. She was surprised to see him home so soon.

"What's going on, Bill? That was a short run. Are you all right?" she asked.

Typically, Bill ran for at least an hour, usually more. He'd been doing this for quite a few years, so she knew this was not his norm.

"I got the worst leg cramps, and they wouldn't go away. My legs are still sore, so I figured I would take a break. I'm also debating whether to go to the doctor or not," Bill responded.

His mom gave him a funny look. "Well, you had a call from the doctor. They said you have an appointment tomorrow morning."

Bill was happy to hear that, as he hadn't realized he had an appointment set up. He figured he had just forgotten to write it down. So, the next day he showed up to his doctor's office, happy to be able to talk to someone about the cramping. However, when he checked in with the receptionist, she told him he didn't have an appointment.

"Oh? Well, that doesn't make sense. Why did I receive a reminder call for an appointment for today?" Bill asked, confused.

She responded nonchalantly, "I couldn't tell you. I didn't call and have no idea what is going on."

"Well, can I get in? I mean I'm here and having an issue, so it was serendipitous that I had an appointment."

"I'm sorry. We are fully booked," the receptionist answered. She said they had no room to squeeze him in, so Bill had no choice but to leave. He was bewildered, but he also knew he had to see someone—it felt important. On his way out of the doctor's office, he all of a sudden got the feeling that his dad was with him. It was the first time Bill had felt his dad since he'd passed. It seemed like he was telling Bill to look across the road.

When Bill looked up, he saw an emergency walk-in clinic and decided to go inside. He felt it was something his dad wanted him to do, and he agreed. Bill checked in and quickly described what was happening. He assumed the doctor would give him a once-over and then prescribe a muscle relaxer or some topical cream to help with the cramping. He was wrong. As it turned out, Bill had a condition called popliteal artery entrapment syndrome. Essentially, his calf muscle was pressing on the artery behind his knee. Without proper treatment, he could die.

Thankfully, Bill followed his dad's nudge to go into the emergency clinic. The doctors there determined that he needed surgery immediately. They got him into the hospital right away and were able to perform the much-needed graft surgery. The first surgery, though it helped initially, soon failed; Bill had to return for a second surgery, which has held up.

Since that fateful day, Bill has continued to exercise. He bikes now, which keeps him healthy and happy. He knows following his intuition, and his dad's direction, literally saved his life. To this day, he doesn't know for sure, but he believes his father was behind that phone call about the mysterious doctor's appointment.

Jim

When he was a rookie police officer, Jim was told by his trainer that if he ever went against his gut reaction, he would regret it. That was proven to him one night while he was walking his post.

It had been a slow night, with not too much going on. It was still early, though, so Jim knew, based on his experience as a cop, that there would be something. That something came in the form of a man Jim found lying under an oil truck. The victim told Jim he had been jumped, beaten and robbed by a group of guys. He whispered the attackers only got fifty-seven cents.

Of course, Jim thought. *Fifty-seven cents. Was it really worth beating this guy?*

"Do you have any idea who they were? Did you hear any of their names?" Jim asked.

The victim responded that he knew one by the nickname Naanaa. Jim had no idea who that was, but he swore to the guy he would track Naanaa down one way or another. Unfortunately, the victim died shortly after being brought to the hospital. Jim knew it was a senseless death. He had to find Naanaa and hold him and his group accountable for murder.

Jim checked with the senior officers and detectives at his station. No one was aware of that name or any references to that name. So, Jim asked his guides and loved ones on the other side to help him find Naanaa by sending him intuitive messages.

A few days later, Jim was walking his beat when he saw a large group hanging out down the street. As he looked at them, he saw an ethereal glow around them; it was almost like they were high-lighted or lit up by the northern lights or something. He knew it had to mean something. Suddenly, Jim got an intuitive flash that the glow was caused by his helpers on the other side, guiding him to the group of guys.

Jim started to approach, knowing his helpers were enhancing his gut instincts. When he got closer, he yelled out, "Hey, Naanaa!"

One of the guys in the group turned around and said, "What?"

Arrest made.

Jim now wonders if it was actually the deceased victim pointing out the group by highlighting them in an ethereal glow. It's such a shame that he had to die for fifty-seven cents, but Jim was thankful he was able to get justice with help from the other side.

Rebecca

Rebecca was trained as a firefighter and was relatively new to the job. She craved the action and excitement—it was something she'd always wanted to do. One day, Rebecca and her fellow firefighters were called to a house because the owner reported a suspicious smell. She was geared up and ready to go, but everyone who had done a walk-through said there was nothing wrong. There was a slightly strange odor, yes, but the homeowners said they'd had a fire in their firepit the night before, so everyone attributed the weak scent to residuals from that.

Suddenly, Rebecca got a very strong sense that something was wrong. She moved toward the living room; she felt like she was being guided there. Everyone asked her what she was doing, and she responded she wasn't sure, but she had a really weird feeling.

Once in the living room, she looked around and didn't see anything suspicious, but she still believed that something was off. She felt pulled toward the entertainment center. It was the type that had solid doors, which were closed to hide the television and other electronics from view. Feeling drawn to the doors, Rebecca opened them and immediately saw what was happening. Unbeknownst to the occupants of the home, one of the electrical wires had gotten caught on a hinge and had stripped. There was slight smoke built up behind the doors, and when she opened the door fully, the wire began to spark.

Had Rebecca not trusted what she was feeling, she and the rest of the firefighters would have left without locating the fire hazard. More than likely, they would have been called back to put out a small fire or—worse—the family's young children may have gotten burned when they went to watch TV later that day.

Rebecca's fellow firefighters gave her a pat on the back and confirmed that listening to spiritual guidance may indeed save her life and the lives of others. We don't always have to know exactly who is helping us, we just have to let them.

Gina

Gina, a mother of two young boys, was driving uphill on the highway. The road was pretty dense with traffic, and she was stuck behind an eighteen-wheeler, but Gina was still having a great morning. She turned up the radio and sang along with her kids, not a care in the world. Then, without warning, she saw a huge tractor trailer wheel careening toward her car, trailing smoke.

In that instant, Gina knew she had to move. But the traffic! The highway was incredibly congested. Instead of panicking, Gina trusted her helpers to clear the way. The car beside Gina swerved toward the side of the road, giving her space to quickly work her way over. Her car was inches from getting smashed by the wheel.

Once Gina was safely in the other lane, the traffic behind her slowed to a crawl almost instantly, avoiding the wheel until it rolled off the side of the highway and out of sight. Gina credits her angels for saving the lives of her and her children as well as the other drivers who were able to narrowly avoid being struck.

Gary

Gary was out and about one day, running mindless but necessary errands. Suddenly, he heard, "Go home!" He looked around, sure someone was yelling at him, but no one in the store was paying him any attention. So, Gary decided to keep shopping, thinking maybe he'd just overheard someone else's conversation. But after taking a few steps, Gary knew without a doubt that that message was for him—he felt like he was being physically tugged to the exit, so much so that he abandoned his cart and went outside.

Once he was outside, Gary saw an image of his house and his father-in-law, who lived with him. It felt like the rest of the parking lot disappeared and he was there, at his house, for a second. Then, he literally felt like he was being tugged to his car. Gary jumped in and drove home, much faster than he should have. When he got there, he ran inside and found his father-in-law lying on the floor, not moving. He immediately called 911 and an ambulance came and took him to the hospital.

When Gary talked with the doctor afterward, she told him that if they had gotten to the hospital one hour later, his father-in-law would not have made it. If Gary hadn't recognized his helpers sending him impressions in several different ways, he would have finished shopping and not gotten home in time. Gary knows it was not his father-in-law's time to go and that his helpers played a key role in keeping him alive.

Stella

Stella, a high school student, had been at a party. After a few hours of chatting and dancing, she was exhausted—she'd been tired before she even went to the party. Finally, Stella decided it was time to leave so she could get home and go to bed. So, she said her goodbyes and got into her car.

Right away, before she even took her car out of park, she figured she would partially roll the windows down to help her stay awake. Once her windows were cracked, she cranked up the music, sang along to the song on the radio, and started her drive.

Stella was about halfway home when she began to feel really sleepy. She shook her head, rolled the windows down the rest of the way, and continued driving. Next thing she knew, she heard, "Wake up! Wake up!" With a start, Stella realized she'd fallen asleep and was currently veering off the side of the road, headed for the gully that ran alongside it. She swerved back on the road and made it home—wide awake the rest of the way.

Stella told me that she knew, without a doubt, that it was her guardian angel that had woken her up, saving her from, at the very least, a bad accident, and probably much worse.

I Get By with a Little Help from My...

As you've read, dreams are not the only way our loved ones, guides, angels, and other helpers show up to assist us. Though dream visits may be the most prevalent for you, your helpers are also around during waking moments. The metaphysical moments you have may be gifts of guidance from your helpers collaborating with your own intuition. It's not necessary to know where intuitive directions are coming from as long as you're able to recognize the impressions.

PRO TIP

Loved ones and helpers and angels, oh my! They may appear in your dreams to guide you.

Chapter 9

INTUITIVE FLASHES AND MANIFESTING

Manifestation is, essentially, the act of bringing something tangible into your life by believing that it can happen. It is about cultivating your energy—trusting that you are living and designing your experiences by focusing on positive outcomes as if they've already come true. It is the creation of what you desire without putting effort into the actual act of creating it. Manifesting may be something you've experienced intentionally—or not. There's no limit to what you can manifest or how often you can manifest something.

We will dive more into manifestation later in the chapter. First, we are going to talk about intuitive flashes.

A Flash of Insight

Have you ever done something, or felt compelled to do something, with no clear reason why? I believe these moments to be intuitive flashes or intuitive events. They don't have to be quantified as a particular intuitive gift; after they occur, we often realize that they were a special mix of intuitive gifts, signs, synchronicities, and even soul directives.

Dr. Harmony

Dr. Harmony has experienced several intuitive flashes. She had a very religious upbringing but knew, intuitively, it was not the path for her. Even after becoming a chiropractor, she found herself drawn to the metaphysical, and she now works in new age healing. She is the author of the award-winning *Twin Flame Ascension* oracle deck. Over the years, Dr. Harmony has followed her soul's directions and let it guide her through many life changes:

> I built my chiropractic practice, but my soul longed for more than just body; I needed to work with all of it: mind, body, spirit, and even the heart. I knew, intuitively, it was part of the path my soul wanted me on. Had I not chosen to change my career, I wouldn't be where I am now—working in the metaphysical energy-healing world.
>
> I continued tuning in to what my soul was trying to share. It was through that experience that I discovered everything is our mirror, our reflection. And that understanding, along with all the other learning along the way, led me to the creation of my *Twin Flame Ascension* oracle deck, which in turn led me to write a book.
>
> By continuing to listen to my soul, purposefully, I am living my best life—my soul's life. I've always known I was meant to teach others to tap into the spiritual rather than religious, and with this following of my intuitive soul's experience, I help to create freedom within myself and others.
>
> —Dr. Harmony

Vanessa

An intuitive flash is a spiritual nudge. Intuitive flashes may present as one of the clairs, but they happen so quickly that you may not even realize it. You may feel guided to do something, or you may even find yourself doing something without realizing it. If this action then helps you in some way, it could have been caused by an intuitive flash. Though it's hard to determine what exactly an intuitive flash is, keep this in mind: if you feel your soul guiding you, but you're not able to easily attribute it to one of the clairs, you're probably experiencing an intuitive flash.

Vanessa, a psychotherapist, was sitting at her desk, working. Her schedule for the day was full of telehealth clients. She kept busy taking notes during her sessions, as usual, but after a few hours, she discovered she had been doing something else without even realizing it: she had made a big ball of tissue.

Sitting there, on top of Vanessa's desk, was the ball. That was unusual, as she normally only had papers and her computer on her desk. Even more perplexing was that the ball was a result of her own making—she had mindlessly balled up unused tissues for no reason. She'd created a five-inch ball. Then, she'd wrapped tape around the tissues in all directions. Even more mind-boggling was that she'd wrapped the tape sticky side out. Vanessa hadn't been cognizant of doing any of this. Once she realized what she'd done, she set the ball on her desk, out of reach.

Later that day, after she was done with all of her client sessions, Vanessa decided to clean out her lowest desk drawer. It was a very deep drawer, and it was packed with stuff. She hadn't cleaned it out in a long time, so there was a lot to go through. Once she was done removing everything from the drawer, she found a layer of pencil shavings and other detritus at the bottom. She tried to remove the drawer—she planned on dumping it out into a garbage can—but the drawer wouldn't budge.

Even though it seemed an impossible task, she was determined to clean out the junk at the bottom of the drawer. She just couldn't figure out how. After about fifteen minutes of trying to gather and remove all of the tiny debris left in the drawer, Vanessa had a light bulb moment. She grabbed her tissue/tape ball and used the sticky tape to collect and remove all of the bits of trash. Vanessa realized, after the fact, that she had been intuitively guided. Without knowing it at the time, she'd been creating this special tool so she could complete a self-appointed mission.

This is a perfect example of a typical intuitive flash: doing something with no idea why you are doing it, only for it to make perfect sense later. You can call it a synchronicity or precognizance, or you can call it what it is: a textbook example of an intuitive flash.

. . . . . . — . . . . . .

PONDER THIS
INTUITIVE FLASHES

Figuring out what your intuition is trying to tell you is more important than distinguishing what kind of gift you are using. We've all experienced intuitive flashes: you may do something for no reason other than that you felt compelled to, or you may feel like you need to make a change, out of the blue, with nothing to back this up other than an instinctual feeling. These are common ways your intuition works through flashes. You may have more than one flash, or it might be one and done. Either way, pay attention to what your intuition is sharing with you!

Lindsay Fauntleroy

Lindsay Fauntleroy is a licensed acupuncturist, the award-winning author of *In Our Element*, and a personal growth healer, among other things. Several years ago, she had a difficult choice to make: go back to school while her baby girl was still in diapers, or continue with her current job and lifestyle. Lindsay knew that going back to school made no sense at that time of her life; she had just about made up her mind when she had an intuitive flash that pushed her to go back to school. She described it as coming out of nowhere, a belief that went against her logic, but she knew it was her intuition, and she couldn't just ignore it:

> Trusting that intuitive push to go back to school turned out to be one of my best decisions. And once I took that step, my destiny took a step toward me. I received a $12,000 scholarship for my first semester. Miraculously, my job was willing to decrease my hours and keep me at the same pay rate.
>
> Doors opened for me that I could not have planned or anticipated. As I took that step forward following my inner compass, more was revealed. Trusting your intuition often requires a leap of faith and an act of trust.
>
> —Lindsay Fauntleroy

Lindsay's path had been practically laid out for her without additional schooling, but then she received the intuitive message that she should go back to school. School turned out to be the exact thing she needed at that point in her life, and it set her up to receive so many additional gifts from the universe. If she hadn't followed her soul's push, she wouldn't be where she is today! Listening to your intuition will absolutely change the trajectory of your life.

Mark and Patricia

Patricia's intuition also changed the direction of her life, though she didn't know it at the time. Her husband, Mark, had an intuitive flash that contributed to hers in a huge way, though neither were aware of their intuitive guidance in the moment. This next story is a combination of Mark's and Patricia's intuition, because one naturally led into the other.

Coming home from a night out, Mark and Patricia pulled into their driveway. Without warning, Mark slammed on his brakes.

"What are you doing?" Patricia hollered as her body crashed forward.

"I'm sorry, honey—but look!"

There was a box turtle standing in the middle of their driveway. Now she understood why he'd stopped so suddenly.

"How'd you even see him? I can barely see him and we're right next to him," Patricia said.

"It's a her, and I'm not sure. I just knew she was there," Mark answered.

"How do you know he's a she?" she laughed.

"I have absolutely no idea, but I also know she's pregnant!" he answered. He wasn't sure what had happened, but he'd had some kind of intuitive flash. He knew to hit the brakes and he knew the turtle was female. He also had a flash of eggs breaking, so he knew she was getting ready to have babies.

Patricia wasn't sure Mark was right, but she was willing to put some effort into it in case he was. They picked the turtle up and created a nesting area to put her in so she would be somewhat protected. They saw her leave two days later, and she didn't come back. They figured she had been looking for a safe place to lay her eggs because they saw she'd dug up the soil in the nesting area they'd made for her. A couple of months later, the babies were hatched, and Patricia brought them to a turtle sanctuary. That was the end of Mark's intuitive flash, but hers was just beginning.

Patricia was so interested in the welfare of "their" turtles that she discovered a new passion. She'd done a lot of work researching and learning about them, and she even began working to protect turtles. In her work, she ended up volunteering for a variety of studies that had to do with turtles.

One such study asked for volunteers to venture into a particular area to collect snails. They were looking for barnacles on the snails, which would indicate whether or not there were diamondback terrapins cohabitating in the area. Of course Patricia volunteered; she was fascinated with all things turtle by now. Unfortunately, all the other volunteers bailed, so Patricia became even more adamant that she needed to participate—it was important.

Patricia grabbed a five-gallon bucket and set out to look for snails. All she needed was the bucket itself, but she had a flash of herself holding the lid, so she took that too. As she wandered off, she regretted bringing the lid—it was just one more thing she had to carry. She didn't need a lid for a bucket that was going to be used to collect snails.

Then, as she closed in on the location where she would begin gathering snails, Patricia got stuck in the mud. It was dense and sticky, what she imagined quicksand would be like. With every attempt at a step, Patricia was sucked in deeper and deeper. Her boots got stuck. She was buried about three feet already. The more she struggled and tried to get out, the more she sank. She'd get one foot out, sans boot, and the other would sink deeper.

Patricia continued this for a few panicked minutes. Then, her intuition suddenly kicked in. It was like a light bulb had gone off. Patricia realized why she had taken the lid! She pulled one foot out and put the lid under it. She was able to pull her other foot out without sinking into the mud. She made it through the mud one foot at a time, using the lid as a platform.

Patricia had experienced an intuitive flash. Initially, she had no idea why she brought the lid with her; it seemed strange, but she felt compelled. She found out later that the quicksand-like mud in that area was twenty feet deep. Patricia has no idea how she would have escaped had she not brought the lid with her.

Dawn

What happens if you ignore your intuitive flashes? Well, you may not have a happy ending. Dawn's family experienced this firsthand. Her grandfather had recently passed away, so Dawn's half sister and niece were driving up to visit. Before they arrived, Dawn had a notion to hide her jewelry box, even though she had no particular reason to feel that way. She thought she was being silly, so she chose not to move it.

After everyone left, Dawn set about straightening up. When she got to her room, she noticed her jewelry box was still there, right where she'd left it. Unfortunately, her grandmother's wedding ring, which she'd inherited after her grandfather died, was not. It was among a few special items that were missing. Though she did confront her half sister, Dawn never got the ring back.

Sherice

Sherice had a similar experience: she didn't trust her intuitive flash until after it came to fruition. It was Sherice's first day back at work after a vacation. It had been a long day and she couldn't wait to get home. As she got into her Jeep, she remembered she had to get gas, but the gas gauge read between a quarter and a half tank, so she decided to postpone the errand so she could get home sooner.

As Sherice was pulling out of the parking lot, she had a flash of riding in a stranger's car. She had no idea what it meant, so she shook it off and headed toward home. As she was getting on the highway, she had another flash of arriving home without her Jeep. Again, she ignored it.

Suddenly, Sherice's Jeep shut down. She managed to coast over to the shoulder of the road. When she came to a stop, she looked at the gas gauge: below empty. That's when, she said, she put all of her intuitive flashes together. Thankfully, she was able to catch a ride home with a Good Samaritan. Then, her boyfriend drove her back to her Jeep, filling up a gas can on the way.

For some reason, Sherice's gas gauge had malfunctioned—it had shown the tank as more full than it really was. Because Sherice was eager to get home, she ignored the multitude of intuitive flashes she received. Luckily, when she ran out of gas, she was able to pull over safely. In that moment, Sherice swore to never again ignore her intuition.

I've made this promise too, but sometimes we don't recognize our intuitive flashes until after the fact.

EXERCISE Ask for a Flash

By now, you know it's possible to receive guidance at any time. The more you ask your intuition for help, the easier it will be.

Read the following questions one at a time and then wait for a flash of insight. The flash doesn't have to leave a big impression; it may simply be a spark of understanding. Let go of the desired outcome and let your intuition work for you!

+ How can I best move forward?
+ What do I need to be successful?
+ How can I live a life I love?

+ Who will help me increase my happiness?
+ What is most important for me to know right now?
+ What do I need to let go of?

Allow the first flash to be your answer, and observe it without judgment. You may hear words or feel something in your body; you might even see images. However your insight shows up is perfect! Any time you need additional guidance, you can ask your intuition questions.

—

You won't always be able to identify intuitive flashes. There is so much happening in our lives that these gifts sometimes get lost in the flurry of activity. Being aware of an intuitive flash can make your life smoother, but it isn't a necessity. I can tell you from my own experience that my senses get my attention when they really need to.

Manifestation

In its most basic form, manifesting is creating something from nothing. What this means for us is that we have an innate power to bring things into our lives, both positive and negative. Think of manifestation as what the mind believes we can achieve. If we believe we can achieve great things, we will, but the opposite is true as well. Your self-talk can unwittingly affect your life and form who you are—thereby manifesting your path. So, it's important to speak kindly about yourself.

EXERCISE Simply Manifest Something

You can manifest anything you desire. The instructions are simple: just follow these rules for a quick guide to manifesting!

- First, think of something you want to manifest.
- Believe you can manifest it. Truly believe it.
- Then, ask for what you want. Yes, ask the universe for what you want!
- Finally, let go of the outcome. Don't try and figure out how something will happen. Just let it happen.

Be open to participating by acknowledging any nudges from your intuition or the universe along the way, but expect the manifestation to happen and leave it alone! It may take a day, a month, or even a year, but keep expecting that your wishes are going to come true.

—

We have the capacity to manifest things like our dream job, financial stability, a loving marriage, and more. We use our intuition all the time, but do we consciously set about to manifest what we desire? Sometimes. Here are some of those intuitive manifesting stories.

Chris

Chris took a seminar course while also working as an engineer. It was a noncredit class with coursework related to the things Chris did in his day-to-day job, as well as some writing exercises. For Chris, one of those writing exercises turned into a manifestation exercise, though he didn't realize it until much later.

Chris's teacher asked them to write a paper for the class. It could be about anything, but it had to be very descriptive. Instead of writing about his usual topic—work—Chris decided to take a different approach.

He sat down and wrote about his perfect partner, describing her in detail. She was dark haired, petite, a skier, a Vermont resident,

Jewish, smart, fun, family-oriented, and plenty of other things Chris wanted in a partner. As he was writing, he totally zoned out and let the words flow out of his hands and onto the paper. He had to reread his own paper to see what he'd written—it had felt like he was channeling it. I believe he was! Chris was channeling the intuitive energy of the universe as he wrote down all the things he wanted in a wife. But he didn't realize that he was, indeed, manifesting at the time.

A few weeks later, Chris's teacher gave him back his paper with a big A written on top. Chris put the paper away and totally forgot about it. A month later, he went out with some of his friends. At one point, he noticed that sitting in front of him was a woman who resembled the perfect partner he had written about. He struck up a conversation, and the more they talked, the more he realized this was the exact woman he'd described. Everything he'd wanted, everything he'd written about in his paper, was a trait that the woman in front of him had. Chris was ecstatic.

Needless to say, Chris asked the woman on a date. They went out and completely hit it off. On their second date, he showed her the paper he'd written about his ideal partner. It described her to a T. She was gobsmacked—and he knew right then and there that he had manifested her. Not long after, Chris proposed, and he and his perfect partner have been together for thirty-four years.

Marion

Marion also manifested her partner—with a little help from her deceased mother. It happened accidentally after Marion repeatedly utilized her intuitive abilities.

The first thing Marion did was ask her mom for a sign that she was around. She specifically asked to see a hummingbird. That way, she'd know her mother heard her and was helping her from the other side. Bam! Out of nowhere, a hummingbird came buzzing up to

Marion's window. It was almost instant, a very quick confirmation, and it made her extremely happy.

Things didn't end there, however. Marion had been wondering what to do for dinner, and right after the hummingbird appeared, she intuitively saw an image of a very specific shrimp dish that she loved. She decided to trust her gut and go get it for dinner. Marion was feeling lucky—not only did she get affirmation her mom was around, but she also loved the food she was being guided to, and the restaurant was easily accessible—it happened to be right across the street!

As Marion was getting ready to go to the restaurant, she wondered when she would get a boyfriend. She'd gone through a rough divorce recently but was feeling ready to get back out there. She was a strong woman, and she was financially independent, but she missed having someone in her life to share things with. So, Marion decided she would manifest a boyfriend.

After she finished getting dressed, Marion walked across the street to the restaurant. Because she was alone, she decided to sit at the bar. Since she was by herself, she had brought a book to read, but it ended up being too dark in the bar area. She thought about getting her meal to-go and heading home, but her intuition told her to stay. She listened and sat at the bar by herself, eating shrimp and drinking wine.

So far, Marion had had a really good day, and set the intention to have a good evening as well. She trusted that her vibes would lead her in the right direction. At that moment, a couple of guys walked in and sat at the bar. Though she didn't know them, Marion instantly felt a strong connection to one of the men. He looked over and started talking to her, and his friends joined in. For a while, Marion hung out with the group; it felt so natural. Plus, she could feel a stir in her belly that had nothing to do with her dinner—her gut instincts had kicked into high gear, and she knew she needed to pay attention.

Eventually, the evening came to an end. As her new friends were getting ready to leave, Marion felt as though she was losing something important. She watched them walk out the door and instantly knew she had to follow them. She had to talk to the man she'd felt a tug toward the whole time.

Without a second thought, Marion followed her instincts and met up with the man outside. Apparently, he had felt a connection as well, and they ended up exchanging phone numbers. Two days later, he went to her house and cooked dinner for her, and the rest is history.

Marion credits her mom for manifesting her boyfriend, since the initial sign that had jump-started her intuition that evening was the hummingbird. She hadn't even been thinking about a boyfriend before her hummingbird showed up, and then everything fell into place.

It's common to call upon our deceased loved ones to help us manifest. When we want something, we have a tendency to ask our loved ones and guides for it. This is still manifestation—we are just getting some assistance from the other side. There's nothing wrong with asking for help from those who knew us best.

Cheryl

Cheryl and her friend decided they wanted to move in together to save on rent. They started looking in an area between where they both currently lived, but they couldn't find an apartment that worked for them. They decided to expand their search area, looking as far as fifteen miles in every direction. Neither Cheryl nor her friend wanted to commute too far, so they compromised by agreeing to the fifteen miles.

Still, they had no luck. There didn't seem to be anything out there that was in the right area *and* within their budget. They were so frustrated they were getting ready to quit looking. Then, someone told them they should manifest the perfect place.

"What do you mean? We've tried! We've been looking everywhere!" Cheryl replied in exasperation.

"I mean both of you should get together and write down exactly what you want. Describe everything in detail. Don't leave anything out. No matter what it is, write it down. Nothing is too small to include," the woman said.

So, Cheryl and her friend set out to manifest their new home. They kept it practical while also listing every single thing they wanted, including the right location, type of building, number of rooms, size of the rooms, amenities, and everything else they could possibly think of. They even wrote down that they wanted a gas stove instead of an electric one and that they wanted a private yard where they could grill and have friends over.

The next day, they went online and looked at listings once again, even though they doubted they'd find anything. But then, unexpectedly, it was like a bright light exploded on the computer. There it was. A new listing, right between where each of them lived, exactly where they wanted to be. It was everything they'd listed on their paper, right down to the backyard. Cheryl and her friend immediately went and looked at the place, and they signed a lease that day! They now know that there is nothing they can't manifest when they really put their minds to it.

Cheryl and her friend doubled up their manifestation power by both contributing to it. Sometimes that extra boost can help create exactly what you want, especially if it's something that involves your friends or family.

Emily

Emily was ready to move. The only problem was her family wasn't really on board. Every time she found a house she thought would work for them, her husband or one of her kids would decide it wasn't right for some reason. Her intuition was telling her it was time, and her family would be super happy in what she knew would be their perfect home. So, she called them all together one night.

"I know we need to buy a new house. This is the only way it is going to happen: we need to manifest it. We have to write down what each of us want. We are all going to live there, so we should all have a say in our new house," Emily explained.

"Mom, we know you're into all this, but come on. We are not going to 'manifest' the perfect house. That's kind of ridiculous, don't you think?" her younger child said.

"Oh, come on, let's try it," her older child said. "It can't hurt!"

"Yeah. Come on, guys. Start giving me some things you definitely have to have in a new home," Emily said.

"POOL!" both kids shouted at the same time.

"Okay, okay. I get it—you want a pool." She wrote it down.

Emily and her family began listing things they really wanted in a new home—even down to the doorbell. At their current place, they didn't have one, and they could never hear if someone was knocking on the mudroom door. As they talked, they got pretty good at the process, and they ended up with a huge list that they then divided into a "must-have" list and a "want to have" list. Obviously, the first thing on the must-have list was a pool. Second were office spaces for both Emily and her husband, preferably separated by French doors or something so they could keep them open when they wanted to talk and close them when they needed to focus.

By the time Emily and her family finished brainstorming, they had written down a lot—these were *very* comprehensive lists. Honestly, Emily thought, they would never find this dream house in their price range. Still, she said, "Let's all focus on everything we wrote down, look at the paper, and hold hands." After they had grabbed hands and formed a circle around the paper, Emily said, "We are manifesting our new home, and so it will be!" They all cheered and threw up their hands.

Even though she was eager to move, Emily decided she would wait until something that fit her family came along. She was surprised she didn't have to wait long—two weeks later, she saw a listing for the perfect house. It had everything on the "must-have" list *and* the "want to have" list. She made an offer right away, and it was accepted. Emily decided to do another family manifestation ceremony to sell their old house quickly. It worked!

Emily listened to her intuition and manifested with her family, both to buy a new house and sell the old one. She knows it took all of their energy to manifest the perfect place.

EXERCISE Manifestation

You can do this manifestation exercise alone or with others. Keep in mind that when you're trying to accommodate multiple people, manifestation can get tricky. However, if you're able to include loved ones in your manifestation ceremony, your manifestation has a better chance of coming to fruition.

+ Write down exactly what you are manifesting. (If you are working with others to manifest something, I recommend asking everyone to write their own list of what they need or want. You can then combine your lists. This will make the process smoother.)

+ Once you know exactly what you will be manifesting, focus on what it is that you want. Ask the universe to bring you what your intuition is telling you that you need. Share how it will help or benefit you and any other interested parties. Visualize this new reality.

+ Thank the universe in advance for manifesting what you want. Then, simply let go. Put your list in a drawer somewhere, or place it under your bed. Try to forget about it. You don't need to know how the universe will make things happen—just trust that it will.

+ Finally—and this may be the most important step—be present in your life! Participate in your life! If an opportunity presents itself, don't immediately disregard it; if it's something your intuition connects with, go for it! It may lead you to exactly what you manifested.

You Can Create a Life You Love

Manifesting a better world for yourself is within reach, especially if it's something you're intentionally working toward. We manifest constantly. More importantly, we can manifest both positive and negative things. Be mindful of the thoughts you have and the words you say out loud—these can bring situations and people into your life whether you are aware of it or not. Instead of putting yourself down or getting hung up on what you don't have, focus on everything positive in your life. This will bring you more of the same, or even better!

PRO TIP

Not all intuitive flashes need to be qualified as a specific clair—just recognize them as your intuition trying to help you. You can also utilize your intuitive gifts when manifesting. Use your intuition to see your best possible life, then manifest the positive opportunities to get there!

CONCLUSION

People are so interesting. Everyone has their own tale to tell. We all own a piece of intuitive history—the only thing holding us back is acknowledging our experiences. It doesn't matter what you do in life, or what family you were born into: intuition is your birthright, and it is something you can and should utilize often.

Intuition can help us in every area of life. We've seen how many people were directed to a new path (or even away from a tumultuous one) in the pages of this book. It should also be noted that some people—myself included—shared stories about how disregarding their intuition had a negative impact on their life. We've seen the outcomes of these situations. Let them be a lesson to us all that even though we may not understand our intuition, when we trust it, we usually have an easier time. Remember, these are real life stories. This is not a novel. Though some of these stories may seem unbelievable, they are 100 percent true, and they should be an inspiration for all of us.

Some people shared stories of crucial moments or events where they had the opportunity to listen to their intuition. They were gifted with the possibility to change their circumstances. It didn't matter if they realized it at the time, or even if they believed in intuition— their connection to their intuition and their knowledge of how it can affect them and those around them was gently (or even forcibly) adjusted. Everyone I spoke to agreed that they now consider it extremely important to pay attention to their psychic impressions.

I want to emphasize, again, that we have all experienced intuitive guidance in some way or another. Quite often, we've experienced it in more than one way. You've read stories of clairvoyance, clairaudience, claircognizance, clairsentience, clairempathy, clairgustance, clairalience, and clairolfaction. I've also dazzled you with true stories of signs and synchronicities, intuitive dreams, and help from deceased loved ones and other guides. Perhaps you have had an intuitive flash or manifested using your intuition.

While reading, you've likely felt drawn to one or two of these gifts, or if you're more in tune, three or four. You may also have felt like the stories you were reading could have been your own stories. Your intuitive intelligence has been expanded in ways you never could have imagined merely by reading about others' experiences. Sensory input, whether it's physical or metaphysical, grows with familiarity. Essentially, the more you use your gifts or are exposed to them, the more your muscle memory will kick in.

Don't feel disappointed or even upset if what you've read about are things you have not yet discovered for yourself. Simply knowing what is possible may help you utilize other abilities. One way to develop your own gifts is to do some of the exercises within the book. Pay attention to those you feel drawn to—this will help you figure out which skills you may be more proficient in than you realize. The exercises that you want to ignore are probably ones that will be more challenging, though they will undoubtedly expand your awareness of all things metaphysical.

With all of that being said, there may be some metaphysical senses you never use; your intuition may not present itself in that way. Find comfort in the fact that the gifts that you personally use can always be further developed. Just because you are more adept at some senses than others doesn't limit you.

Perhaps you have read this entire book and have no desire to do any of the exercises. However you chose to enjoy this book is totally fine! Maybe you wanted to learn something new, or maybe you simply wanted to be entertained; both are valid. It's also possible that you wanted to feel connected to people who have had similar experiences. Perhaps you've felt unable to share your intuitive stories with friends or family for fear of judgment. Learning that other people have had situations like yours can give you that kindred feeling.

I've absolutely loved collecting these stories because it has shown me that people actually *do* put stock in their metaphysical senses, as they should. It's also been fun to see the light bulb moment when someone discovers they were following their intuition without even realizing it. As I've talked to others, I have learned that every life has an effect on every other life. If we are going with the flow, following our soul's guidance system, it has an impact—no matter how small—on everyone around us. Conversely, if we are going against the flow, those around us feel the effects, and more often than not it leads to a grating experience for all. When you think about it, intuition works in pretty much the same way as the butterfly effect: it leads to changes that are felt all over the world in some way and, in fact, it can and will change outcomes.

It is my wish that you walk away from this book with a bit of awe, some new know-how, plenty of insight, and a lot of curiosity. Stay real and stay intuitive!

RECOMMENDED READING

Auryn, Mat. *Mastering Magick: A Course in Spellcasting for the Psychic Witch*. Woodbury, MN: Llewellyn Publications, 2022.

Baron-Reid, Collette. *Uncharted: The Journey through Uncertainty to Infinite Possibility*. Carlsbad, CA: Hay House, 2016.

Crow, Granddaughter. *Belief, Being, and Beyond: Your Journey to Questioning Ideas, Deconstructing Concepts & Healing from Harmful Belief Systems*. Woodbury, MN: Llewellyn Publications, 2022.

———. *Wisdom of the Natural World: Spiritual and Practical Teachings from Plants, Animals & Mother Earth*. Woodbury, MN: Llewellyn Publications, 2021.

Dale, Cyndi, ed. *Root Chakra: Your First Energy Center Simplified and Applied*. Woodbury, MN: Llewellyn Publications, 2023.

Dawn, Awyn. *Paganism on Parole: Connecting to the Magic All Around*. Woodbury, MN: Llewellyn Publications, 2022.

DeNicola, Alison. *Auspicious Symbols for Luck and Healing Oracle Deck*. Illustrated by Sabina Espinet. Stamford, CT: U. S. Games Systems, 2022.

Dr. Harmony. *Twin Flame Ascension: Take Me Home Oracle Card Deck*. Stamford, CT: U. S. Games Systems, 2022.

Fauntleroy, Lindsay. *In Our Element: Using the Five Elements as Soul Medicine to Unleash Your Personal Power*. Woodbury, MN: Llewellyn Publications, 2022.

Holland, John. *Bridging Two Realms: Learn to Communicate with Your Loved Ones on the Other-Side*. Carlsbad, CA: Hay House, 2018.

Margolis, Char. *You Are Psychic: 7 Steps to Discover Your Own Psychic Abilities*. New York: St. Martins Essentials, 2022.

Matlin, Jenna. *Will You Give Me a Reading?: What You Need to Read Tarot with Confidence*. Woodbury, MN: Llewellyn Publications, 2022.

Nelson, Tammy. *Integrative Sex & Couples Therapy: A Therapist's Guide to New and Innovative Approaches*. Eau Claire, WI: PESI Publishing & Media, 2020.

Robinett, Kristy. *Embrace Your Empathy: Make Sensitivity Your Strength*. Woodbury, MN: Llewellyn Publications, 2022.

Rooney, Lisa Anne. *A Survival Guide for Those Who Have Psychic Abilities and Don't Know What to Do With Them*. Woodbury, MN: Llewellyn Publications, 2018.

Wix, Angela A. *The Secret Psychic: Embrace the Magic of Subtle Intuition, Natural Spirit Communication, and Your Hidden Spiritual Life*. Woodbury, MN: Llewellyn Publications, 2022.

To Write to the Author

If you wish to contact the author or would like more information about this book, please write to the author in care of Llewellyn Worldwide Ltd. and we will forward your request. Both the author and publisher appreciate hearing from you and learning of your enjoyment of this book and how it has helped you. Llewellyn Worldwide Ltd. cannot guarantee that every letter written to the author can be answered, but all will be forwarded. Please write to:

Melanie Barnum
⁒ Llewellyn Worldwide
2143 Wooddale Drive
Woodbury, MN 55125-2989

Please enclose a self-addressed stamped envelope for reply,
or $1.00 to cover costs. If outside the U.S.A., enclose
an international postal reply coupon.

Many of Llewellyn's authors have websites with additional information and resources. For more information,
please visit our website at http://www.llewellyn.com.